# WHEN THE MIRACLE
# DROPS

# WHEN THE MIRACLE
# DROPS

## HOW INSTAGRAM HELPED TURN A QUICK FIX INTO
## A MILLION-DOLLAR PRODUCT

by
Jesseca Dupart

*Printed in the United States of America*

First Printing, 2019

ISBN 978-1-9990240-0-0

Book Design by
**www.designisreborn.com**

*A WritersBlok production with editor Izabela Szydlo*

# DEDICATION

~೦೦೦~

When the Miracle Drops is dedicated to the little girl who believed she could and actually did it, Baby Jess, and to the entrepreneur who will take him or her present and future self very seriously when reading this book.

# THANK YOU

Thank you to all parties connected to Kaleidoscope's growth. That includes the people who were a part of Kaleidoscope in any way: my people, the stylists and barbers who worked in my salon, the individual contractors who sold Kaleidoscope Hair Products, those who worked in the warehouse and all the influencers.

# FOREWORD

mir·a·cle
/ˈmirək(ə)l/
Noun

1.  a surprising and welcome event that is not explicable
    by natural or scientific laws and is therefore
    considered to be the work of a divine agency.

Jesseca Dupart, aka @DaRealBBJudy, is many things:
mother, friend, entrepreneur and social media sensation to
name a few. What she is not is selfish. This is the way Jesseca
has been able to experience many miracles in her own life.
From using all her savings to open Kaleidoscope Hair Studio
because she trusted her vision and rebuilding (and launching
Kaleidoscope Hair Products) when a fire devastated the shop
a few months after it opened to finding the strength to take
her business to Houston when her family was split up because
of Hurricane Katrina and trusting that the Lord would keep
them safe, Jesseca's faith has kept her going—and yielded her
miracles. In turn, she has become almost superhuman when
it comes to giving and helping create miracles for others! Over
the years, Jesseca has given an overabundance of gifts,
donations and resources for the betterment and growth of the
community. Mostly recently, she became part of a group that
holds the Guinness World Record for the largest toy
giveaway.

Jesseca has also done speaking tours in several cities to share her knowledge of how to build, grow and maintain a business. Now, she is sharing that knowledge and more in this book. Jesseca invites you to live your best life by taking advantage of all the roads she's already traveled, curating a customized experience by your hand, all the while providing encouragement along the way. From the first chapter, you will be hooked, inspired and in tune with your vision more than ever before. This book is really a road map to your personal success.

So often in life, it's easier to believe miracles for others, but Jesseca invites you to experience them for yourself. By the end of this read, you should be ready for your personal miracle to drop! Don't stop there, though. Please take a page from Jesseca's book—literally—and pass it on!

*Niecy Nash*

# TABLE OF CONTENTS

# WHEN THE MIRACLE DROPS

# Chapter 1

## INTRODUCTION

Growing up, I didn't see many CEOs who looked like me. They mostly all wore tailored suits, had neatly-trimmed hair and carried briefcases. But the reserved businessmen with money I grew up seeing are not the CEOs of today. Now, people—including myself—are breaking all the rules and expectations of what CEOs are. I see CEOs who wear flip-flops or, in my case, the most incredible hairstyles you'll ever see, and get deep in the trenches with their team. They aren't afraid and are willing to take chances. Social media has definitely helped by spotlighting different types of CEOs and leaders. Thanks to this online world, as the CEO of Kaleidoscope Hair Products (KHP) I can stand next to the president of a big box store as proof that anyone can be leader and head a million-dollar business. Social media has created a level playing field. It's just about how you market yourself.

Within yourself, you already have everything to manifest all your dreams, goals and hopes. Through this book, I want to support you in achieving them! As you read, you'll learn how to:

- affirm your current goals and identify your passion;
- develop goals for your future;
- tackle your doubts head-on and seek direction from the Divine;
- adopt a CEO mentality and understand your unique selling point;
- establish a strategy for business and marketing success; and
- engage with your social media audience.

## THERE IS NO ROOM FOR DOUBT

One of the biggest myths about me is that I came out of nowhere. People look at my following and how fast KHP popped and think my success happened easily and overnight. They don't see the work and struggle that made it possible. Being pegged an overnight success has to be one of the most common misconceptions, overall, of being a successful entrepreneur in today's social media age. Rather than wondering how they can step their game up, people wonder why they aren't making it big or why they're not getting rich as fast as others appear to be. By doing this, they eventually get discouraged and give up. I'm going to say it straight for you: There is no such thing as an overnight success. Success is achieved through hard work, staying on top of your game and trusting the vision God put in your path.

People are going to doubt your vision and ability to get from where you're currently at to running a successful business. These people will be your family, friends, acquaintances or even those you consider your ride or die squad. When they doubt you, you are gonna listen and a part of you, the part you assume is rational, will think, "Thank the Lord I have them to keep me from doing something stupid like spending my hard-earned money." The other part, the stubborn and illogical part, is gonna say, "Screw that! What do they know?" When those conflicting voices enter your mind, you must learn to throw out other people's logic. Those people love you but they don't have your vision and your gift from God. They don't see what you see because this isn't their path or purpose. It isn't that they doubt you because they don't believe in you. They could think you're the smartest person they know, but that doesn't mean they're going to be on the same path as you.

Listen, my momma and daddy wanted me to become a doctor or a lawyer. To them, those were paths that would make me financially secure, allow me to have a comfortable life, and bring me success and joy. They didn't understand hairstyling. Back when I started, nobody was doing hair the way we do it now. My parents didn't have a frame of reference for understanding my dreams or that, for me, success was always going to be connected to hair.

Understand this truth: Sometimes, people hold us back because they only know what they know. People can only see things from where they are. And if they're still in the same place they have been for many years, they won't be able to envision something new. You want them to believe in the path God blessed you with? Show them your vision by creating a business so powerful that you're able to share your blessings with those who matter.

I've been doing hair for as long as I can remember. My first client was my dad, who would patiently sit for hours while I played with his hair as a child. As I got older, I started playing with my friends' hair, doing whatever was trendy at that time and coming up with unique styles. I didn't really know what I was doing but I had fun experimenting, playing with styles and seeing how they looked on my friends. I remember being in high school and sneaking my friend Nycole into the house, just to do her hair. I would style hair during any free time I had, on weekends or whenever my parents weren't home. My parents weren't particularly happy with this since they hoped I would use all my time to study. Don't get me wrong, it's not like they shut it down or tried to get rid of my hair stuff but they still held out hope that I'd become a surgeon. Besides, I think my mom hated trying to get all that hair out of our carpet (sorry, mom).

Despite my parents wishing I'd take the known road, they now get it and support me. And I never forget that when I started doing hair professionally, I did it out of my room. Given these humble beginnings, I could have stopped then. I could have given up on the vision of what I knew my life was supposed to be and followed someone else's dream for me. I could have let doubt win and taken the safe route.

Here's a little visualization exercise I want you to do. Imagine your vision, whatever it is and whatever form it takes. I want you to think about it and really picture it, in color. Give it as much detail as you can.

| My Ideal Day | Details |
| --- | --- |
| **Who is beside me?** | *Who's sharing this future life with you? Is it friends, family, someone you haven't met yet (a future partner perhaps)?* |
| **What am I doing when I wake up?** | *Are you checking your agenda? Doing yoga? Making breakfast for your family? Going for a jog?* |
| **How am I spending the day?** | *What are you doing that makes the day better? Are you in meetings? Working for a client? At a photo shoot?* |
| **Where am I calling home?** | *Where do you live? In the city, suburbs or country? How does your home look? Is it a house or an apartment? What is the layout and décor?* |
| **How are you getting around?** | *Are you driving a car? Biking everywhere? Walking?* |
| **What else?** | *Include any other information that will help you make your ideal day seem real.* |

Write down these details or grab some photos that inspire you. You're creating the beginnings of your vision board (I'll touch on this more later). I want you to start to imagine this vision as the life you're already living.

You can't change your current circumstances by doing the same things over and over again. If you let fears and doubts hold you back, that vision is nothing but a fantasy. But if you start to believe that it's possible to make the vision real, you're already on your way there.

Now, imagine what can happen if you take that vision further and trust the purpose God put in you. If you take a chance and move towards it, one of two things can happen. You'll stay where you're currently at or you'll live a more fulfilling life than you could have ever dreamed. But you can't move forward unless you trust the path laid out in front of you. Is it going to be straightforward and easy? Nah. But if you believe in your purpose, seek guidance and pray, and put in the work (no matter what it takes), you'll achieve heights beyond what you can imagine.

The question now becomes, are you ready to commit to your vision? When you do, the path becomes clearer and those hurdles that could have broken you will be stories you share about your faith and perseverance.

Let me tell you how trusting my vision played out. In 2013, I opened my first salon. It was a big deal. The space was bright, vibrant, and most importantly, it was mine. It also represented my personality, hard work, dedication and sacrifice. December of that year was our busiest time and it was also when we lost everything in a fire. Kaleidoscope had only been running for less than six months and everything was gone in one day. We had eager clients but no equipment or space. Even when we did secure a workspace, we didn't have supplies to serve our clients. That was a really tough time but before we knew it, we had received an abundant outpouring of love and donations from the community.

We reopened Kaleidoscope Hair Studio in April 2014. By this time though, I had realized I wanted more. I decided to relaunch Kaleidoscope in July 2014 as a salon that also offered the quality hair products my customers needed. I'm gonna be straight with you. It would've been easier to walk away or just rebuild to where I had been before the fire because business was doing well. Instead, I took that moment to think about what I wanted and trusted in the vision God showed me. I started again by moving away from what was safe and familiar and embracing something new that I was certain we needed in the marketplace. Oh, and you know how people always say it takes a lot of money? Well, there are actually many brands starting right up with hardly any capital. Honestly, it just takes persistence, creativity and time. I started Kaleidoscope Hair Studio with $2,000 to my name and a whole lot of faith.

I'm stressing the importance of staying dedicated to your vision and not doubting your path because there will be so many people telling you "no" that you'll need to learn to tell yourself "yes"—constantly. Yes, I have this dream. Yes, I can make this dream a reality. Yes, I am creating the life I am meant to lead. You gotta have that conviction because if you doubt every single decision and move you make, your mind will be filled with so much negative energy there won't be any room for His vision. Begin your journey by saying, "yes" to your dreams.

## Jesseca to Judy (@darealbbjudy)

Let me back up a bit because my professional hair journey really starts in high school. While I wasn't overly involved in school because I had my first child at 15 and my priorities naturally shifted, it was this period in my life that really ignited my passion to do hair professionally. In the ninth grade, I started off on a partial scholarship but was put out. I transferred to another school that also wanted me to leave and told my parents that if I left the expulsion wouldn't be on my record. During this time, I had tested for Benjamin Franklin High School, one of the best schools in the city. The officials there didn't want me because the school had never had a pregnant student. My parents, though, weren't about to let anything stop me from attending. They fought for me to stay and I did but eventually transferred again, this time to John McDonogh High School. John Mac, as everyone knew it, was one of the worst schools in the city. But the one thing it did have was the best cosmetology program in Nola. Because of that, going there was a no-brainer.

When I left Benjamin Franklin, I was in advanced placement. So, I only had to complete Honors English and I could use the rest of my time to get the hours I needed for my cosmetology license. While John Mac gave me my start, in 2003 it made the news for more horrific reasons. That year, two men with an AK-47 and a semi-automatic killed a student. As students tried to escape, some were hurt. Among them was a pregnant senior who was trampled. The shooting happened only a year after I left, so hearing about it was really scary. Beyond that, police raids at the school weren't uncommon. In fact, on my first day there was a raid, complete with drug-sniffing police dogs checking bags and lockers. I didn't grow up in this world and had never seen this, so I was like, "What the hell is happening?" As people were

8

getting arrested, I was like, "Shit, this is the worst decision I ever made." But I wanted my cosmetology license, and no police dogs and drug dealers were going to stop me. In fact, these events quickly made me realize I didn't want to live that lifestyle and made me even more driven to succeed.

During high school, I took hairstyling from hobby to hustle. I would charge $25 and do the most ghetto, high and hard hairstyles for the popular girls. I didn't approach these girls; they came to me to create something that would make each of them stand out. I guess you could say they were my very first collaboration with influencers, minus the Instagram part. After that, I kept doing hair at my mom's house—from the very same room I had shared with my sister.

While I was a trailblazer of sorts in high school and I felt like I was really doing it on my own, there were definitely people I looked up to and turned to for mentorship. Finding a mentor and people to draw inspiration from is crucial in your journey. You'll be surprised who you can learn from.

Identify some skills you think you need for your business and who you (person or brand) immediately associate with each skill. If it's a person you know, reach out and ask him or her to share his or her knowledge. Asking for advice can be as simple as going for coffee to chat or setting up an informal business meeting. If a brand or celebrity comes to mind, study how they engage with their followers and audiences, and check out any of their books, articles, interviews or talks. Make sure one of the people or brands you have included is a leader in your industry.

Below are some crucial skills for brands in the digital age. See who comes to mind and add to what I've started.

| Skill I Need for My Business | Who is Great at This? | How Can I Learn from Them? |
|---|---|---|
| Social media | | |
| Sales | | |
| Video editing | | |
| Photography | | |
| Industry leadership | | |

A few years after high school, I was at the top of my game. Even though I was co-owner of a shop, I really wanted to set myself apart. As I kept looking at social media, I was thinking, "I'm better than some of these people with 60,000 followers." The thing about social media is that you're no longer competing with your neighborhood; you're in competition with the world. So, when people see my Instagram profile, they're not comparing it to another New Orleans stylist; they're looking at all the hottest stylists, whether in New York or Sydney, Australia.

I took that interest in social media and decided I wanted to reach people outside of New Orleans and be the best for hair online. I made these my goals and started to create Judy, my online persona, who is now part of all my marketing campaigns from Judy Springer to Judy Wonka. I noticed that one hair influencer I followed at the time wasn't taking the opportunity to build and further monetize on her success. She wasn't selling any hair products or anything. That was something I knew I could do by not limiting myself. "I can do this," I thought, "and create products and content that will appeal to people in every city." When I got to 100,000 followers, I didn't stop. Instead, I looked around to figure out my next goal. Another influencer in my industry had a million followers. At that point, it almost felt natural to go, "Well, if I can do 100K, why can't I do a million?"

There was nothing malicious in these goals. I didn't try to ruin anyone's reputation or attack my competition. I wasn't even jealous of them. I took the work of these influencers as an honest challenge to myself and approached it with a "if they did it, why can't I?" attitude. It's the same mantra I want anyone looking at my page to adopt: "I can beat Jesseca!" And, of course, you can try. But the thing about being an entrepreneur is if you don't do anything then nothing happens. You're not in a nine-to-five job where you can sit around and still get paid or clock out and not think about work. You have to be on top of your business 24/7 and be proactive to get stuff done. There is no one else to fall back on. There is only you.

## READINESS CHECK

For the questions below, I want you to write down the first names or ideas that come to mind. There is no judgment here. Whatever your first answer is, write it down.

**Who will support me?**
*E.g. My mom*

> **How can I leverage the support?**
> *E.g. Speak with her when I need clarity, advice or a sounding board*

**Who will create doubt in me?**
*E.g. My old boss*

> **What can I do to keep their doubts from stopping me?**
> *E.g. Remind myself that no one but me has to see the vision the Lord has for me*

**What will keep me motivated?**
*E.g. Meeting other entrepreneurs*

> **Who will hold me accountable?**
> *E.g. My friend Stacey*

**What will make me want to give up?**
*E.g. Getting discouraged if my first 10 posts don't go viral*

**How can I stay motivated?**
*E.g. Remind myself that building a lasting brand takes time and look to people such as Jesseca for inspiration*

**How will I hold myself financially accountable?**
*E.g. Pay myself first*

**Who and/or what is holding me back?**

What?

Who?

**Does the person who is holding me back have a new place in my life?**

Be very mindful of who you bring forward with you 'cause when negativity is using up all the air, positive things can't grow.

## DISCOVERING DIVINE DIFFERENCES

I always knew my path in life was going to be different. When I started doing hair, there wasn't anybody who did it like me. What I didn't know at the time was how to get my business the attention it deserved. That changed in July 2014.

When we reopened Kaleidoscope Hair Studio and launched our product line, I hired a popular hair stylist to be a special guest at the event. I saw the immediate impact, on my sales and social media followers, of her posting and talking about it. I took the lesson and recognized the importance of social media to my brand. Since then, social media, especially Instagram, has become instrumental in building my success. So much of where Kaleidoscope is today is a direct result of how I've been able to get the brand across to different people through various online platforms.

Let's be real though, having social media and using social media are two different things. And, recognizing how powerful a solid social media strategy can be is not the same as having one. When the studio burned down, we created a GoFundMe page to help us get supplies to keep the business going. Our goal was something like $2,500 and we raised $550. This is a perfect example of how we didn't have a real understanding of what online presence and social media marketing could do or how we needed to strategize to drive engagement and business.

As an Instagram influencer, people assume I picked up my phone and the likes and follows just materialized. My first post was in June 2012 and it had 200 likes thanks to my friend Supa Cent, owner of the makeup brand The Crayon Case. Supa has supported me from the very beginning and was the first person

I collaborated with. Working with her, I saw opportunities for both of us to take advantage of each other's follower counts.

To effectively use social media, you need to stand apart from all the other people doing the same thing as you. People make this a lot more complicated than it is. The bottom line is if you want to be different, be you! There is no one as interesting, unique and powerful as you. God made only one of you, so why are you trying to be someone else?

Don't compare yourself to someone else's success, journey or status. Not only is that depressing as hell but it's also the most useless activity. Comparison is very, very discouraging and distracting, but even worse, it can stop you from being creative. When you're starting out and you compare every idea with a veteran's, yeah, theirs might look better, but yours might be funnier, more engaging or realer. You're not going to post that idea if all you see are the ways you think it's lacking. Also, when you keep watching others, your ideas are bound to get jumbled up with somebody else's. That will turn your original and creative ideas to a copy of someone else's thoughts. You see it all over Instagram. For example, a picture in a trendy coffee shop of a pretty latte and an open computer with the hashtags #work #hustle #life. That idea was fresh and different the first time someone did it. Now, so many feeds are just this image on repeat.

Seeing the boost from my work with the hair stylist encouraged me to go after other influencers such as Tokyo Vanity of Love and Hip-Hop fame. It was a collaboration that got almost 1,500 likes. I went from averaging around 500 likes to three times that amount in less than three months. How? I was doing something no one else was doing in the industry at that time: I bartered my hair skills for mentions in people's posts.

Combine that with my love of color, and suddenly, my Instagram feed was giving people a different experience. They knew on my page, they would see color, famous faces and humor. This concept of originality should apply to all aspects of your life but especially marketing.

This was my difference—my personality, my humor and my drive. In short, me. I thank God daily for who I am because I know He doesn't make any mistakes and He made me just right, with the ability to share His message through me. Kaleidoscope is the same way. We aren't trying to be some other company. Because of that, I always try different approaches to keep things fresh and new.

When we launched our most successful product, Miracle Drops, we had a couple of choices. We could be very clinical and informative but dry, or we could try something a little bit more distinct. How do you speak about alopecia considering that for a lot of people, it's a very sensitive topic? People don't want to admit they're losing hair, let alone have someone else tell them. I wanted to curate a unique experience that involved joy and laughter, so I talked about it with humor. Kaleidoscope's differences are what make us exciting and fun to follow.

My most significant change on Instagram occurred when I did a series called The Edge Police. Supa and I dressed up like police officers, and in real time, ran up on real people, telling them how bad their hair looked and how we could save it. It could have gone really badly and we could have gotten hurt, so both of us were terrified. But I knew it was a risk that could pay off big time—which it did. I grew my Instagram following and shifted my entire career. It worked because the content was unique and authentically Judy.

Recognizing divine differences is about understanding the way your life is shifting and how those changes will open doors and create opportunities. But be aware, not all your original ideas will work out or be viral hits. That's part of the process and you have to continue to trust in your uniqueness and challenge yourself to experiment.

My friend Shiggy, for example, has been doing skits and honing his craft for years on Instagram with The Shiggy Show. This man was trying new stuff when one of his challenges went viral. He had followers, but it took just one thing to bring a lot more awareness. When the #InMyFeelingsChallenge and #DoTheShiggyChallenge went viral, everyone felt like he came out of nowhere. Nope, that man had already been hustling, creating, and generating new ideas and unique content to connect with his audience. Shiggy always challenged himself, but he also never changed who he was or what he enjoyed doing. His divine difference was his ability to use movement, music and comedy to express himself. He wasn't being anyone but Shiggy — and it worked.

Another area where your differences matter is in how you define success. When I first started, my definition of success was what everyone had on their social media: nice cars, fancy watches and big houses. As Kaleidoscope grew, so did my definition of success. It became associated with gratitude rather than material things.

So, if you asked me in 2013 what success was, I would have said having my own shop, where I could make my own decisions and the moves I wanted. I had a shop before, but I shared that with a partner and when I got to the top of that game, I knew it wasn't going to be enough for me. Today, if you ask me what success is, I'll tell you it's happiness and doing something you love while inspiring others to grow. I look at success now in relation to the impact I have on people. If I die tomorrow, did I grow brands that help other people? Can I meet God and say I used His gifts as He wanted me to? Remember this, success isn't just monetary. Money can't always get you what you want.

## WHO RUNS THE WORLD? LEADERSHIP LESSONS

I've always been a fan of Oprah and Beyoncé. These are two powerful and strong women who run successful empires but are still authentic, give back to the community and refuse to give into what is socially acceptable.

Like the lack of CEOs who looked like me, there also weren't a lot of faces like mine on TV when I was growing up. But there was Oprah, this successful TV host who was in control of her money and her image and had a staff working under her. I used to watch her every day. The thing that fascinated me about Oprah was not just that she had achieved success but that she was the boss. She had a team of men and women who looked to her and trusted her to lead them. For a young girl in the South, that was almost surreal. Without emphasizing race too much here and getting into that larger conversation, it was just about realizing that it was possible to be a leader and be successful. The other thing I really admire about Oprah is that she knew the right time to bow out. She ended The Oprah Winfrey Show at the height of its success. She didn't wait until it was on the decline but rather stepped down when she was ready to launch her OWN channel. I appreciate her attention to market details. She left on a high note, took a calculated risk and launched a new brand. Oprah lives her life with no regrets and pushes her brand to continually evolve and grow.

Oprah has also accepted that with success comes responsibility. From the stories she shares to the philanthropic work she does, Oprah is all about helping and inspiring people to get to where she is. For example, on her show Oprah's Master Class, she straight up gives you the tools and lessons to level up, to move forward on your path and to achieve success. Oprah gives away so much of what she makes as well. She's said that when she dies, her money will go to charity because she doesn't have any children and there are so many people she wants to help. This is someone who is fulfilling her purpose and serving her higher self. From Oprah, I take away many lessons about leading and community building. She was the first of my kind of CEO, an African American woman who changed the conversation around not just what Black women could be but also what leaders are.

There are many reasons why Beyoncé is the queen, but the one I want to touch on is her amazing ability to strategize and command the industry on her own terms. Beyoncé is synonymous with hustle; the woman is always moving and creating. I remember hearing that when she came back after her first maternity break to record a new album, she had more than 300 songs for the label to hear. While she had focused on spending time with her baby, she was also evolving and decided to incorporate her roles as a woman, mother, wife and performer into her work.

When all the attention was on what happened between Solange and Jay-Z in the elevator after the 2014 Met Gala, Beyoncé didn't say a word, which is actually a crucial piece of advice Oprah gave her. However, she went on tour and revealed to fans the whole story, singing her version of events and taking ownership of her narrative. She wasn't going to let someone else speak for her. Her team has also played a role in ensuring that Beyoncé is the only one to tell her story. She put together a great team, which reinforces the idea that effective leaders must be surrounded by people they trust. Her team carefully controls the messaging to guarantee you're focusing on what they want you to focus on, whether it's a song, an album or a video. Though the burden of leading and navigating difficult situations may be on the leader, having a solid team makes you a stronger leader and enables you to effectively handle any crisis.

As a leader, your team and a lot of other people are counting on you. Because it's like being the head of the household, you can't shift your problems onto someone else. Yours is the final word on solving those problems. You're also the person people look up to, fall back on and call on. That can be very overwhelming at times. The double-edged sword is that you can't let the people who depend on you see when you're overwhelmed because you don't want them to lose faith in you and the brand. It's absolutely crucial to adopt a never give up mindset. If you give up then your team will give up. You must never allow that to happen.

Beyoncé also understands the difference between Beyoncé the product and Beyoncé the person, keeping both separate until she wants to share parts of her personal life. She knows how to capitalize on her life and strategically utilize it to drive her sales and business, without letting society get too deep into her private business.

Social media drives Kaleidoscope's popularity because it's the brand's main marketing avenue. This means I have to stay on top of my social media game, from trends and the newest hashtags to viral videos. Sometimes, the content creation choices are easy, like when I asked Shiggy to be on Judy Springer. But even then, I have to watch what's happening on social media. Right before he was set to come on with his girlfriend, Shiggy publicly apologized to her for cheating. The story, though not connected to Kaleidoscope, had the potential to impact the brand and take over our collab. So, I had to monitor it to mitigate any risks, which may have meant canceling the show with Shiggy and his girlfriend. Luckily, we shot the episode and it was successful, but as a leader, I'm always aware and making sure that the Kaleidoscope brand is telling the story we want to share with the world.

Taking hold of every opportunity is another Beyoncé lesson. Just because things don't go your way doesn't mean you let that stop you. I don't stay still. It makes me itchy and gets on my nerves, driving me to try something new. That's why if I'm going out of town for work and for some reason that trip is a fail, I don't go back to the hotel and chill. I figure out how I can seize the opportunity and create something from it. If I have my videographer or photographer with me, we may do an impromptu photo shoot. If I can schedule a meeting, I will. Because I always come ready to work, if something isn't happening, I will make it happen.

I can't talk about Black CEOs without giving a shout out to my friend Supa who I met on social media, started collaborating with on projects and watched grow into a millionaire CEO with a hugely successful makeup line in less than one year. I look at my friend, see her business decisions and her savvy mind, and I'm like, "Damn, I know this person." There is something especially amazing about watching your friend take over and build an empire. Seeing her evolution is both inspiring and humbling.

This visionary, who saw a need in the market to introduce not just a new makeup line but also a new way of applying makeup, amazes me. She changed the industry by helping people become more comfortable with difficult makeup techniques without sacrificing who she is as a person. I laugh sometimes because she is this makeup maven, but you'll see Supa on her Instagram story without makeup, hair in a cap, wearing casual, comfy baggy clothes. She isn't about creating and maintaining a fake image of someone who's always Instagram-ready. Supa's business grew really quickly, but she's stayed true to who she is: a little hood and completely real.

Seeing her growth also humbles me because it reminds me of how people view my story. We are two women who, statistically, shouldn't have made it being that we don't have any formal education. Now, both of us are leading multi-million-dollar businesses.

In different ways, these three strong leaders and Black women showed me that your mindset will determine how you carry yourself and your brand. I remember when I went into retail stores, I was excited and then realized I needed to start thinking about storage and keeping product in stock to fill the demand. I could easily have said, "It's okay if I fail because I just don't know." But that wouldn't have been the mindset of a CEO, so I stepped into the thought process of the leader I wanted to be. I started to think that I could do this and tackled the challenge instead of letting the challenge take me down.

There's one particularly important lesson in being a leader that I want you to internalize. You never arrive. I know people think that once they get to a certain point, they can coast because they've arrived. Arrived at what? I'm never sure. Hate to burst your bubble, but as an entrepreneur, you're always en route to "arriving". I may get an order for $1 million today but that's just today. I need to figure out how I'm going to top that tomorrow. How am I bringing in $2 million? You must always be improving your personal best.

Here are your first lessons for building a successful business, which we'll look at in more detail throughout the book.

- **Understand your brand:** Understand not only the value you are bringing to the marketplace but also the difference, whether it's in experience, marketing or the product. Stay on top of that advantage and make it work for you.

- **Tell your story or someone else will:** As a CEO and leader, you must always be in control of the messages that impact your brand, whether they come directly from you or from others. When it comes to incidents that may not reflect well on your brand, be ready to address it but only when you're prepared and have consistent messaging.

- **Failure doesn't mean you can't hustle:** Life will always throw unexpected events your way. The deal you thought was solid might fall through after you have traveled to meet the client, the person you were going to collaborate with could cancel, and on and on. Though it sucks, these moments are your chance to network, hustle and find different business opportunities, regardless of circumstances.

- **There is need to pretend:** Being someone else all the time is exhausting, even if it's only on social media. You want followers who genuinely connect with you so let them see your authentic and creative side. Let them meet the "real" you, flaws, no makeup days and all.

- **Mindset determines the outcome:** Your mindset is the most important part of being a leader. Draw strength and faith from God and never give up. If it helps you, create a daily affirmation.

- **You never arrive:** There is no magical moment when a heavenly chorus sings, "You have aa-rrrivedddd,Ä¶!" The more you make, the more you have to hustle to consistently match or beat what you did the previous day. Never stop working.

## A FOUNDATION CALLED FAITH

I understand and embrace that I'm here because of God's blessings, and I'll never take that for granted. What I enjoy most about what is I do is being able to positively impact many lives. God gave me this platform to speak about my experiences and support people. I love to hear how my story or prayers helped clients and other business owners.

In truth, we all want to be guided and we all want success. When people see someone who is successful, they want to imitate him or her. So, it is our collective responsibility to ensure we don't lead each other down the wrong path. The U Better Get This FREE Knowledge tour I went on in 2018 was about passing my sincere knowledge to those who wanted to change their life. This book continues that. I want you to find your purpose and the path God had laid out for you. I continuously ask myself, "What does God want me to do? What does God want this to be?" I encourage you to do the same.

Since He has given me the platform and all of the blessings that come with it, why would I take advantage of it and manipulate people to choose a direction that wouldn't benefit them? Being Christian isn't something I do once a week on Sunday morning; it plays a large part in guiding my work. The blessings I have are all from Him but so are the struggles. When I'm lost, I pray through the process and ask for His wisdom and guidance. So, when people say, "I look up to you. You inspire me", I know it's because God put me in their path to move them in the right direction.

Faith and prayer are as much a foundation for my work as they are for my life. Both of my parents are very religious. My dad is Catholic and my mom is Baptist. Though I grew up going to Catholic school, at 16 I converted to the Baptist denomination.

Prayer was an essential part of the Dupart household. At Catholic school, on top of religion classes, we went to church every Friday morning. At home, we went to church on Sundays. These church visits were our opportunity to connect with God and ask Him for advice and guidance. My mom instilled that early on, when she would tell us to pray about our concerns. She introduced the Lord as someone who cared and listened and someone who you should listen to. I learned that if I was still, I'd find answers to my questions in the most unexpected ways such as friends I hadn't spoken to in years suddenly calling and giving me the knowledge I'd been seeking. It was this direct connection to God that led me to convert. In Catholicism, even though I was listening to and learning the Lord's words, I didn't feel connected. The prayers felt more like a routine as opposed to genuinely coming from my heart. Although Catholicism wasn't for me, that doesn't mean it isn't for you. Faith is what you feel when your heat is connected to God and your purpose so that it may guide your actions. The way in which you choose to do that is between you and God.

Though I converted in my teens, I only recently began to take it seriously. I've always prayed and believed in God, but I hadn't fully opened myself to Him. I knew I had a higher calling, but I wasn't ready to receive His blessings. That's the thing about faith and prayer, God is on the other side of the door, but you have to be willing to open it and let Him in. As God entered, my path became clearer, and at the same time, I learned how to pray for people. By speaking into people's lives something that helps and supports them, I'm able to seek His guidance for them and for myself.

Before 2018, I would say that I prayed to keep from going to hell. Now, I pray to connect to God and to move myself to a higher level. I am truly saved and I am proud to be saved. My prayers are no longer concerned with the afterlife but about what I am doing here and how I can make my time here better. I also recently began fasting, which has further connected me with God.

People always wonder if there's a verse or a part of the Bible I go to when I'm in doubt but I simply open myself to His word. Having faith is being attuned because God's sly like that. He'll send you signs even when you're not looking. Recently, I received a text from someone I haven't spoken to in more than two years. She is unaware of any challenges I'm facing, but her text said something like, "God told me to tell you that everything is going to be fine. You can go ahead and make that decision." I knew this message was from God, reminding me that as long as I stay on this path He will give me His blessing and He will have my back.

What's interesting about developing my relationship with God is how much it has changed my idea of "the dream". Originally, I had your typical American dream grounded in material wealth. Now, my American dream flows from a spiritual place. Some people are chasing other people's lives, and I want to tell you that you won't get anywhere running after somebody else's dream. Mimicking someone else's life will only bring unhappiness. Trust that God has a unique vision and path for you. You just have to be ready to embrace it. And while God has something greater for everyone, you need to understand that greater doesn't always mean more money. It will, however, always be greater in terms of you being happy and at peace. When you accept God as part of your journey, you'll also soon start to notice the everyday miracles He's creating for you and how they can serve others. At the end of the day, I know all these gifts that connect me to people and allow to me be successful (my marketing, the chemical formula or increased sales) are part of His blessings.

Prayer is the most powerful and selfless act we can perform for each other. It reaffirms our connection to each other, to the world around us and to the Most High. It reminds us to be gracious, humble and kind. Through prayer and fasting, I've met some powerful, strong and spiritual women. There is this wonderful woman, named Veronica, who works at my warehouse. I fasted with Veronica for my business. I knew she had things going on but didn't know what. One day, I messaged her saying I needed to change our meet-up time. She texted me back right away to apologize and say she wouldn't be able to make the new time because her son just had brain surgery. Veronica is the mother of five children, one of whom has cancer. I stood there in awe that she had thought of my needs despite her own fears and worries. I couldn't believe that we weren't fasting for her son. So, every three days, I fast with this beautiful soul, who always shows up ready to help me.

To work from faith, you need to pursue His will rather than act on selfish intentions. Most people tend to pray when things are bad, when they need something or when they're really scared. I'm not saying that's bad because I especially want you to find God during those times so He can be your rock. But I also challenge you to pray when things are good. It's a way to practice gratitude for all the blessings He has given you. When I pray during the good times, I think, "God, I don't want you to take this away. I don't want my attitude to change, I don't. I like this situation. I like what's going on and I just wanna make sure that I am grounded in You."

With success, it's easy to fall off track. I don't even mean through doing drugs or living a certain lifestyle. I mean by no longer holding onto the kind of person you were or wanted to become and instead sacrificing your morals and values for the next like. That kind of change kills people's soul and when all the fame is gone, they need the most love and help. This is the reason I make sure God is at the center of all I do and create. I believe in Him to get me where I need to be in my business and my life.

I always think of life and growth as going up in an elevator. As you progress in life, you get ready for the challenges and opportunities on the next floor. I want my elevator to be constantly moving up so when I pray, I say, "God tell me whatever it is I need to do to stay on the third floor, and if we're going to the fourth, let me be prepared." He and I are moving up, rooted in His word, as one. When He thinks I'm ready, then we'll move up together. Until then, He is helping me grow and evolve to meet the challenges that I'll encounter on the next floor. If you're not focused and you're not rooted in the word, you'll miss some great opportunities. That's why praying in both good and bad times is essential. You need to be close to God at both ends of the spectrum, in joy and in sadness.

When you're grounded in God, all the negative voices, back talk and stuff people say isn't going to matter. People are always going to talk and focusing on them does you more harm than anything. If you don't want to be distracted from your path, here are some things to consider:

1. Stop telling people what you're doing. Your vision is from God, and people may not have the ability to see it and may confuse you with their distracting talk.

2. If people are sharing their opinion about what you're doing but God gave you the vision, recognize that it's just a test of your faith. The stronger your faith, the better the outcome.

Nowadays, people want approval for everything they do. They crave that validation when they're in doubt about their path and the Lord's vision for them. But if you believe something will work because that idea was put in you, trust it and your potential to execute it. If I went into the details of building a car, only other car lovers will get it, but even then, they may not be able to see my vision for changes I want to make to the engine. Your personal vision is similar. If people could understand and do it, they would've done it already and been successful. Your idea is new and different, and it takes a while for people to catch onto new ideas. When I first started bartering, 97 percent of people didn't understand it. They were telling me not to do it but I still wanted to—win, lose or draw. It led to some huge online successes and many of those early collaborators are still my friends, connecting me with new opportunities today.

Without trust in His vision, I'd still be looking at a limited path. He opened up a bigger path for me that included a vision of how to serve Him and others. So, I'm not ashamed to speak about my faith, my belief in Him and the fact that God is the cornerstone of all my work. I'm confident in building my business with His guidance. Creating a multi-million-dollar business wasn't simple. It took hard work, faith in myself, trust in God, and a whole lot of conscious and strategic planning to get to where I am. However, if you're willing to work for your dreams and follow the path that God laid out for you then everything is possible. There is nothing stopping you but you.

**Remember...**

**You don't need permission.**
**You just have to believe and go for it!**

Before you read the rest of the book, I want to say how glad I am that you've chosen to follow your purpose and passion. Don't look to this book to give you permission 'cause only you can give yourself permission to succeed, to follow your dreams and path, and to believe in the vision He has for you.

- Create a daily affirmation (or a few) to remind yourself how powerful you are and where you want to be. It can be as simple or as complex as you want. Here's an example of one:

*"I have the courage to chase my dreams because I can feel His will guiding my way. If I have faith and hustle, there is nothing that can stop me. I will achieve my purpose!"*

**Write yours below:**

# Chapter 2

## IN GOD I TRUST

God is at the center of everything I do. It's my faith in His vision for me, and my life, that's kept me grounded and going during my most challenging times. I know some of y'all are going to read this and say, "Jesseca, that's easy for you to say. You have so many blessings. When have you struggled?" The truth is that everyone, without exception, has demons to face and times of crisis when the only answer is to look to the Lord for help. Recently, someone who previously caused me a lot of grief and pain has been trying to gain a foothold back into my life. The person is trying to connect with my family and people I know and thinks he has a right to be a part of my life. I talk to God everyday about this person, asking why He brought him back into my life and what I should do. I seek God out even in the small details of life.

I can also hear some people saying, "God doesn't help me!" I wanna ask those of you who say that, have you honestly opened your heart to Him and listened? You can't hear His answer when you already think you know what it is. A lot of us think we aren't worthy of His love because we messed up in the past or because we think we aren't good, smart, kind, giving or pretty enough, among a slew of other reasons. We think He made a mistake with us. But He is just waiting for you to ask Him genuine questions from the heart, without fear or assumptions, so He can give you His answer.

Because I was brought up in the church, there was never a point when I felt like I didn't have God in my life. After I became Baptist, I knew I was saved but those words didn't mean much to me for a long time. Accepting Him in my heart and trusting Him to guide my ship were two different things. Even though I knew God loved me, I felt His blessings and I was grateful, I hadn't yet surrendered to His will. I let doubt and fear seep in. I refused to let go, put my concerns in His hands and whisper my wishes in His ear. There was no sudden moment when I felt His presence more strongly; it was a gradual awakening. As I prayed, I felt His presence more and more and became confident in it.

A few years ago, through a toxic relationship, I found my strength and began to understand that He is always with me. The guy wasn't abusive or anything, but it wasn't a good relationship for me. I was depressed. Because I hadn't yet come into my own strength, I equated love with making the other person the center of my world. My boyfriend at the time wasn't about that. He wasn't used to a love that wound you up so tight you were always together. One day he told me, "You need to find a group of friends and stop calling on me so much." It broke something in me. He wasn't unkind when he told me and he didn't belittle me, but the words still hurt.

All I could think was that I wasn't enough. I'd mull it over like, "Why doesn't he want to be around me? Why isn't the person I'm supposed to be building a life with interested in my day-to-day? What's going on?" These thoughts would spiral, racing around my head and consistently making me feel worse about myself. Eventually, I found myself in my room, door locked, hiding under the covers. I felt terrible. My self-esteem was gone and with it, my ability to face the world. I don't know what made me do it (maybe the Lord was looking out for me even though I wasn't ready to pay attention) but I turned on some gospel music. I let the words resonate with my soul and it felt like someone calling me out of the darkness, reminding me I had someone to lean on. Not only did I find a joyful peace but I also discovered the strength to walk away from a relationship that wasn't giving me what I needed.

I'm a forgiving and optimistic person, and I always think people are going to change for the better. So, when I'm with someone, I'll forgive and give more chances than the relationship probably deserves. Finding my strength in the Lord reaffirmed that I was okay on my own and that I needed to save my love for the relationships that matter, instead of clinging to ones not meant for me. I bear no ill thoughts towards that relationship. I came out of it stronger and more connected to God. I know it was meant to teach me that rather than putting so much into other people, I should invest that energy in myself.

The closer I got to God, the better things got. As I mentioned, a major key is praying in both bad and good times—especially the good times. Those tend to be the moments you get distracted and lose focus, and the devil is just waiting to make his entrance. He's coming in to mess with all the good things you've created and cause you to lose an opportunity.

When I started my business, I wanted to be successful. That's it. It seemed so simple. I had this great product and I was going to make it a success because so many people needed it. Here's the funny thing though, as you and your business grow, you realize success is just a way to get to your real purpose. I love helping people, and what success has given me is a significant platform from which to spread my message. We live in a world filled with so much negativity, and I want to be a person who leaves behind a positive mark. God was with me as I created this positive platform. He was there, teaching me how to move forward and create something that was not just a product but rather a community of love and strength. He will be with me as I use the colors He gave me to leave behind a vibrant footprint.

## A CONNECTION FOR DIRECTION

Everyone out there has a great idea, but so many people are afraid to try because that requires taking risks and possibly failing, which is scary. What they don't realize is those failures are the price you pay to grow, to move forward and to learn the lessons that will set you up to win. I took a lot of losses to get my win but when I got it, it was so big that none of my losses mattered anymore. If you're a prayerful person and God puts an idea in your head, you've just got to go with it. Put your feet to the ground and start moving. Knowing that you have a purpose, a goal, something that was given to you will keep you going even when your sales are low or your social media isn't tracking. Have faith and trust in the process.

Everyone has a process. It doesn't matter whether yours is growing a business, building a healthy relationship or becoming a better person, I say this over and over: You have to pray through the process. I'll expand on this later in the book. It doesn't matter who you are, to succeed you need to have a healthy relationship with God, especially when things start moving. When you embrace God and His blessings, the speed at which your life changes will amaze you.

As humans, we're taught to count on other people. But the truth is, most people aren't reliable and the ones who are aren't always available. Even your best friend will have days she won't be around. It won't be her fault and she'll feel really bad about it, but you'll have to stand on your own. For many of you, this is gonna sound scary as all hell. But take comfort in knowing He is with you and those moments are God's way of showing you your inner strength. He allows you to feel alone so you understand that you don't have to count on this person or that person. He is with you. There will be days when humanity lets you down, but there will never come a day when you're standing without Him.

When I meet people and talk to them about their dreams, the first thing they usually tell me is what their friends think they're good at and could make money doing or what they are good at followed by the fact that their friends or partner don't think it's a great idea. I always ask them, "Does your friend know you better than you know yourself? Better than your Creator?" It's human nature for people to look to their peers and friends for advice. However, if your friend is working a nine-to-five beside you, he or she probably isn't the best person to give advice about the entrepreneurial hustle. That friend might have some knowledge and good intentions but he or she is still at that nine-to-five. Really though, the conversation should be between you and God. He has trusted you with a purpose, and now you need to believe that He will reward your hard work and faith. Stop looking for validation.

You might be fortunate enough to know a successful entrepreneur you can approach for advice and suggestions. Remember, even if that person has achieved a level of success, his or her words aren't absolute truth. That person can share his or her journey and personal secrets to success and support you, but your journey is your own. Sometimes, the stories might be good but the lessons in them won't apply to you. My lessons won't always apply to you, either. When you feel lost and confused, look within yourself to determine what seems natural for you. You may find the Divine has already left the answer in you.

Mentors can be great. They can help connect you to your purpose when you're struggling to see it, be your cheering section, and challenge you to explore questions about yourself and where you're heading. Sometimes, we worry about not being able to connect with someone we want to seek mentorship from. To that I say, what's stopping you? In today's connected community, you can reach out to different people over many different platforms. Instagram, Facebook and Twitter all allow you to privately or publicly message someone. Even if that person doesn't become your mentor, I guarantee he or she will at least try to answer your question. Social media is also significant when it comes to mentors because it helps you find out more about the person, her or his values and ideals, and what she or he considers essential.

A mentor is your sounding board and someone who offers advice in a safe space. For that reason, it can be beneficial to find a mentor in your industry. That person can give you excellent inside knowledge and stop you from making industry blunders. It's this type of honest teaching that's really valuable, especially when it prevents or corrects errors that you and your team overlook because they've been part of your behavior for so long. I had one of my advisors once tell me, "You know, you're cursing too much. You aren't hood. I know some of your friends are but you're not. You might want to get it together." This person was trying to get me to realize that unless I dropped the habit, I wouldn't get to the level I wanted to play at. My advisor's comment was my check.

Because a mentor is someone who pushes you and helps you advance your business, one of the hardest things about having one is recognizing when the mentor-mentee relationship has run its course. I had this great mentor; we got along well and he supported me when I started my business. As my business expanded, I began to notice I had outgrown him and what he could teach me. Nothing is lacking in this individual and he remains in my life. But the relationship stopped fulfilling the need it was created for, so I no longer seek his advice as a mentor. In this, you also need to trust God to show you the way.

I've always believed God places mentors in your life. He will send you the right teachers to help you along your path, knowing that when the time is right, you can both move onto your separate journeys. Also, keep in mind that a mentor can lead you in a terrible direction and it may or may not be intentional. Sometimes, a mentor is there to test your resolve and faith in your vision. Feel out your mentor and make sure you are both in the same spiritual space. Otherwise, you might be wasting time. Trust the instinct the Lord gave you, feel out the right direction for you and then recognize when you're ready to cut the cord.

It's also crucial to understand the difference between a mentor and someone who just knows their stuff but can't actually serve as your mentor. In 2018, my business interests were expanding and changing. I started venturing into real estate and as that happened, I found myself speaking to my accountant more. Because his friend is the owner of my building, I also went to him for real estate-related guidance. However, because my accountant represents Kaleidoscope and I'm one of his clients, I don't consider him my mentor. A mentor shouldn't have a direct interest in your company because you want to be sure the advice you get is the best thing for you rather than for him or her. In other words, no one whose advice could have a self-serving purpose should mentor you. I might also have a conversation about the business with a significant other. Though life partners aren't always in your industry, you can decide whether the experience and knowledge they bring to the discussion is valuable. Mentors and guidance come in various forms and fulfill various needs. These people are another way to connect to the Divine and hear His message.

On the flip side, just 'cause you hear the Lord's voice revealing your path and vision doesn't mean everyone else does. I can't tell you the number of times people come up to me and tell me how great it is to see a Black Baptist/Christian/Catholic girl making it in life. Then they go on to tell me how I can better live the Lord's truth. I always think, "Who are you to tell me about my relationship with God, to scrutinize and judge the conversations that He and I have?" They think being saved means they have somehow found their way to the Promised Land and it's their divine duty to make sure everyone who gets in is as righteous as them. I don't mean any disrespect but you know the ones I'm talking about, the ones so caught up in their jealousy that they're more interested in hurting others than healing themselves.

This lesson is probably one of the hardest in this book because it requires acceptance, which sounds deceptively simple but can be challenging. When these types of people start telling me all the things I should be doing and everything I'm doing wrong, I just let it go. I don't defend myself on Instagram or anywhere else people try to call me out for not being "Christian enough". There will always be people who try to get a reaction out of you, and once you engage, you'll be battling small minds all day.

When I was younger, there were only two types of Christians, the perfect ones and the bad ones. You either walked the path of Christ and did everything right—no swearing, no drinking, no mistakes—or you failed. There was no in-between. I used to envy my momma's relationship with God. She used to go to Bible study, Sunday school and deacon meetings. My momma was in church five days out of the week, and I thought that to be a real Christian and for God to speak to me, I needed to be like her.

In my effort to find Him, I tried to be everyone else's definition of a perfect Christian. And by working so hard to be like someone else, I didn't create room in my heart to accept myself as I was. If I couldn't accept that God would see me as perfect, where did I leave any room to hear Him tell me so? I'm saying this because I know a lot of y'all feel like you're not perfect or good enough for God's love and protection. That is a myth. As I grew up, I began to understand that everyone has a unique journey and relationship with God. Your relationship with God is just between you two. If, for example, you curse when you know you aren't supposed to, that's your growth process. When you're rooted in God, you can be confident that you'll weather any storm.

## PERMISSION TO PURSUE PASSION

For as long as I've been helping people, it's always been funny to me how people are all looking for permission—permission to start a business, to go after that promotion, to ask out that hot guy or girl. I'm going to give you that permission: Pursue your passion, your dreams, the thing that makes you nervous, scared and excited at the same time.

I'm sure you read that last line and said, "What's up with that, Jesseca? I wasn't asking for your permission! It doesn't work like that." Exactly. I can give you advice and some tips, but only you can decide to move forward with your passion. It doesn't matter if it's me, your friend or your family members, you don't need permission from any of us to start your future.

People also always ask me what they can do to be successful. I always respond by asking them what they're passionate about. If you can't tell me what makes you smile, laugh or excites you then the question isn't, "What can I do to be more successful?" The question is, "What would I like to be successful in?" I can't give you the answer because your passion is personal.

I'm pretty sure no one wakes up in the morning and says, "I want to be a social media influencer" (or maybe they do but they usually find themselves seeking another purpose). Rather, they want to be successful business owners and the influencer part plays a crucial role in that. To do that, you want to stick who you are—even though being you for the world to see is crazy scary. Your first followers will likely be your friends and family, the people who know you and what you're about. Then, you start to expand your following to strangers and it gets more frightening. During these moments, rely on your faith, your certainty that God made you perfect and your understanding that He has already armed you with what you need to take over the world.

While being you is essential, when you first get in the game sometimes you do have to play by some of the rules — at least until you learn how to break them. Starting out, people often want to imitate established Instagram celebrities, see the hashtags they're using, and understand which photos get the most likes or how they're selling their products. Even I would look at the bigger Instagram personalities to see how I could brand myself in ways that would position me to connect with them.

I wanted to get into the same circles as the influencers I was trying to network with, which meant changing the approach I took to fashion, makeup and lifestyle. I reinvested in my brand and hired a stylist because I noticed that people didn't think I was serious about my business or didn't respect me as a businesswoman. It has been my experience that for a lot of African Americans, respect comes from the type of clothes we wear, the car we drive and the jewelry we own. Though, unfortunately, that's often how people identify success, you sometimes have to give yourself permission to play that game to get ahead. While doing that, though, you still need find authentic elements and integrate them into your strategy. Yeah, I needed to step my fashion game up, but I didn't just copy what the Kardashians were wearing. My stylist helped me work on my personal style and image.

Give yourself permission to grow as a business owner. People are concerned with selling out and being called out for changing, but life is about progression. I have friends I've known a long time, and while I may not have the same time for them as I used to, I'll always be there for them. Some of these friends take that as a sign that I've grown too big and forgotten where I come from. But I'm just focused on my hustle and running a business that has more than 20 employees counting on me.

The more you work to establish yourself, the more your friends will shift. Sometimes you also have to make the hard decision to change your friends. You're going to be grinding 24/7, hustling to make sales and connections to set up your next win. Friends and family won't always understand why you can't pick up their call. They'll fail to realize your lack of reply has nothing to do with them but rather with being focused on something business-related. You may be trying to figure out how to get your budget down and stressing about the next quarter, and picking up the phone at that moment could be extremely draining. Your priorities are going to change, as they should. It has nothing to do with being better than anyone and everything to do with trying to close the deal and keep the business going. Don't let anyone tell you otherwise.

As you grow your business, you'll also have to leave some people behind. While they fit into your old life, they may not align with who you are now or you may begin to see who they really are. I'm not going to drop any names but I used to have a really close friend, who I had known for years. I considered her my sister, my BFF. I later found out she was going to my ex and telling him all about the things I was doing. My ex and I didn't part on good terms and even if we did, there was no reason to be sharing my business like that. I saw the situation as a lesson from God. He was showing me this girl had never really been my friend. If she was acting like this with my ex, I couldn't count on her to keep my secrets or my others friends' secrets. We were working on projects that involved us signing non-disclosure agreements (NDAs) and what she told my ex would risk future deals for us. Once, I was at a celebrity's house and something happened that made us worry TMZ would be interested in the information. It had to stay there, between us. My friend didn't even understand that. Her inability to keep my confidence in relationships and with work meant it was time for her to go. She had no place in the future I was creating.

Your concerns also end up changing. The amount of time you spend talking about the workplace increases and day-to-day conversations become different. As I became an influencer and built my brand, I soon realized I'd have to manage a lot of my concerns on my own and I wouldn't be able to share my business frustrations with my old friends. Let me give you an example. A friend reached out to talk to me about how she was being denied a $5-raise at work. In my head, I was trying to figure out how to renegotiate a deal in which I was offered $1.5 million for something that was worth $1.7 million. I listened and gave her advice about getting that raise, but how was I going to complain to her about a $200,000 loss? It seemed petty after what she had shared and an unfair conversation to have—even though, as a business owner, it would have been a completely legitimate one.

I was clearly in transition from one life to another, from who I was to who I was becoming. During this time, I wasn't lonely. But I was missing a connection to a network of people who understood my struggles as a business owner and could offer some advice. Nobody had yet done anything similar to what I was doing. That's one of the main reasons I wanted to write this book. All the stuff I went through cost me really highly, emotionally and mentally. Longing for peers who were in the same kind of business or went through the same struggles was one of the hardest parts of my journey. As my social media presence increased, I found new friends and social media connections who faced similar obstacles and were also trying to understand how to grow a business without any prior experience. I saw that I wasn't alone in how my priorities were changing and my focus got more intense.

If you're always looking for people to give you permission to chase your dreams, you're also going to look to those same people to give you permission to grow. They, however, won't always want you to grow, maybe because they are jealous, but mainly because your growth will change your relationship and they're afraid they'll lose you. So, they'll talk about you becoming too big to hang out with them. Every once in a while, I hear stuff about me like, "Oh, she's doesn't answer her phone anymore" or "she doesn't look our way when she passes the barbershop." If I'm passing that way, it means I'm on my way somewhere. I'm not focused on stopping and saying hi. I'll chill with you when I have time, but that doesn't mean every time I'm in your hood. At some point, you need to stop being concerned about what people are saying and focus on where you're heading, literally and figuratively. Waiting for people to give you permission at every level of your growth or to catch up to you is gonna be exhausting, and trust me, you have no time for that. Your job is to focus on the bigger picture of your vision, not get caught in the petty fears of others. Trust God to remove those who don't belong in your life and make way for those who will support and grow with you.

## MEANING IN THE MISSION

As I've moved closer and closer to God, I've found clarity in my mission and how I utilize my platform. I want my legacy to be one of positivity and change. Every step I take is with the goal of creating something better and staying connected to my purpose. Finding God amplifies your blessings. He will open doors you never knew existed and show you paths you had never imagined. I'm still amazed by what He is doing for my business and me.

Before you say it's easy for me, I'm gonna stop you. You don't know what's happening in my life. Christians, we're not supposed to judge anyone because we don't know anyone's journey and where he or she is in that journey. God gave me this platform to share my journey with you. You also may have seen my journey and watched my blessings overflow as I became closer to Him. Since you likely saw it from the start, you can't say, "Oh, she's blessed because she's been close to God." No, that's not my story. My story is going from ratchet and cussing to becoming mature, more Christian. My story goes from sharing my gratitude and preaching about it to turning it into a whole movement. My story is that as my Christian life grows, so do my blessings. And that's something I know the world is supposed to see.

I never saw myself as any type of prayer warrior but when I pray, I can feel His presence guiding and teaching me. When people ask me to pray for them, we pray together and I can feel something touching me. I think they feel it too. The majority of the time, they start crying and then I start crying because some block has been moved out of their way, and at that moment, they have a clear connection to God. The trick, though, is keeping that connection once they leave. It's the same with this book. I can tell you all the positive ways I can see the Lord working for people and how He has impacted my life. You'll read these words and be moved, and hopefully inspired, to ask the Divine for guidance. Maybe you'll do it the next day and the day after that. Eventually, though, if you don't see immediate results, you may stop praying again.

There is this quote my friend Niecy Nash had on her Instagram that I think is perfect: "The day you plant the seed is not the day you eat the fruit." Often in life, we're willing to wait for the perfect time, the perfect man, the perfect moment. But with prayer, our patience lasts a few days and then we become skeptical of Him and our purpose. Asking God to share His vision with you isn't going to come without hurdles and tests of faith and love. He is preparing you to withstand any storm that comes your way, so how will you be ready if you shy away at the first sound of thunder?

How do you open your heart to God and your purpose? There is no one sure path. Everyone has his or her own way to connect, and you may need to try a few things before something clicks for you. Know this, all those "failed attempts" are taking you closer to finding the path to your purpose, which will be as unique to you as the path you took to find it. I have friends who use daily affirmations and others who meditate. These methods work for my friends as they connect to God, but just as I said there was no right way to be a Christian, there is no right way to pray.

I have conversations with God, I ask Him the questions I'm struggling with and I listen to His answers. I've also started sitting in reflection to express my gratitude for everything I've accomplished with His guidance. Celebrating my success was hard for me, so it involved a lot of digging deep to take stock of how far I've come. Honestly, there are days I sit there amazed at how much my life has changed, and I have to pat myself on the back and say, "Do you realize what you just did? What you just accomplished?" This isn't something that happens every day, but it's something that reminds me to embrace the next level of my growth.

I call these moments when God is bringing you to the next floor in your growth, leveling up. He will always move you up, whether or not you're ready, so you better be getting ready. It's about embracing and embarking on the next thing you're meant to do, and that's been happening more and more for me. My life has become filled with new adventures, opportunities and moments of self-discovery. Every part of my journey, especially the trials and challenges, prepare me for what's next. Through prayer and reflection, I know I'm ready for the next level, the next challenge. He has made me ready.

Another thing I'm big on is visualization, especially for the success of Kaleidoscope Hair Products (KHP). My visualization is always focused on someone who is better than me. Let me explain. In New Orleans, that, for example, has meant going into the neighborhoods with $5-million homes and visualizing owning one of them. I didn't necessarily want the $5-million home or could afford it at that point, but I needed to see what my future would be like if I kept going. It reminded me that there was still so much to get.

It's important to note that visualization isn't the same as comparison. When we compare, we feel unmotivated. When we visualize, we think of how we're going to get from the point we are at to where we want to be. You know the old adage "comparison is the thief of joy"? Comparison is also the thief of peace of mind and your worst enemy. You don't know how someone got to the place he or she is are currently at and you don't know the sacrifices he or she made. So, the point of visualization isn't to figure that out and envy it. It may take some practice but you'll eventually be able to visualize without comparing.

There's always somebody who's doing way better than you, but there's also always people doing way worse than you. Social media may have you thinking otherwise though because most people just show the good. You forget that people experience the bad when all you see the controlled content so people post. Many see KHP and think that once I started it, I had no issues and the business only went up. But when we were first going into stores, the company actually faced a pretty significant financial setback. We were having a hard time getting our products into stores and our sales dipped 30 to 40 percent. It was a tough time for me. I wasn't sure the business was going to make it. I was terrified sales would decline to zero and we would flat line.

All this was happening at a time when I was also facing personal issues. I was ending a relationship with someone, and we had been sharing a home. He refused to move out even though I had my three kids with me and he was alone. I had no choice but to move into my momma's home. She didn't have enough rooms for us, so I put my kids in one room and I slept on the sofa. I'm still grateful my mom took us in, but at the same time, it definitely wasn't a comfortable situation. I was trying to buy out my ex as I was dealing with a decline in sales. I eventually had a conversation with God, laid it all out and admitted, "I just don't know what to do."

Feeling like you hit rock bottom leaves you no choice but to learn to move past the things that brought you there. Since you know what you were doing isn't working, you can try a completely new approach. I remember thinking, "Well, forget what I did. What can I do? What should I do?" Trusting in my vision, I started to reexamine the problem I was passionate about solving. Then I wondered how I could share my knowledge.

A large part of that knowledge sharing is in the message—and how you deliver it. It's interesting that even when people believe they have a unique purpose, they don't always think they have a unique message. You do though, and how you choose to share it should be authentically you. Because laughter helps me manage all the uncertainty, fears and trials life throws at me, it's the way I share my truth. My messages are all wrapped in humor. The way I figure it, the Lord made me funny for a reason, so might as well use that gift as a vehicle to share my passion.

As with social media posts, if your delivery just mimics how someone else delivers his or her message, it's be a watered down, irrelevant version that will bring in watered down results. Keeping your messaging fresh is important, especially as you establish your brand and business. Some of my craziest ideas have gotten me the furthest. I just had to take a chance and try them. Recently, I turned over management of my business social media accounts to a marketing team, but I still check the posts every week to tell them what works and doesn't work. It's not that the marketing team isn't good. It's that there are certain elements, words and image combinations that work for my brand and others that don't. A generic format used by other hair product companies just isn't going to make sense for KHP.

The bigger your brand becomes the more people trust you and feel a sense of community with your brand. Your responsibility to ensure the brand is retaining its core values and messaging will become even more critical. As more people get involved, it will seem easier to let others take on the marketing or communications, but the accountability for messaging and resulting sales always lies with you — the founder, owner and face of the brand. You've got to continue to hustle even when you're winning. Remember, there is no such thing as arriving 'cause you're always working towards your next move, hustle and payday.

## EMPOWERED ENTREPRENEURSHIP

Once you live in your purpose, all things will fall into place. God's plan is more significant than you can ever imagine.

With personal growth, your vision will grow as well. The idea you start with, like opening a hair salon, will definitely not be the end vision. If you asked me last year, I would have said my path has evolved to being the CEO of a hair product company and a social media influencer. If you ask me this year, I'm a CEO, an influencer, a property manager, a speaker for God's truth, a mentor and teacher, and an author. Ask me again in a few years and I know that vision will have evolved some more.

You are unique and powerful! No one else can do what you can do. There hundreds of hair product companies in the world, but what makes Kaleidoscope unique is my personality. Who I am has impacted who I hire, the products I sell and the overall energy of the brand. So, despite a saturated market, Miracle Drops are unique because they work and are creatively marketed. Instagram allows you a choice of influencers to follow but none are like me. The success I've achieved comes from being me and no one else. And, yes, as I grew and my vision changed, the company also evolved because I paid attention to things that would advance it to the next level of growth.

As a female entrepreneur, you always have to be on top of your game. People, especially some businessmen, are going to look for ways to make your accomplishments appear smaller than they are. It's easier for them to believe that you are some puppet beauty queen being propped up by some man than believe you did all this on your own. The way some men will not respect the business side of me is my biggest annoyance. A while ago, we worked with a male performer. The deal was done, and I went to shoot a video with him and his team. As soon as he met me, he was like, "Tell me who your sponsor is, 'cause I know you're not doing all of this by yourself." It's frustrating to feel everything you've worked for being undercut by some stupid comment. My only sponsor is God, and everything I do is a result of a lot of hard work.

When they aren't disrespecting you, they're trying to shoot their shot. So, they either don't take you seriously or they ruin a working relationship because they can't get with you. A while ago, I flew out — and by "flew out" I mean bought a ticket, spent my business dollars and gave my limited time — to meet this guy. He was someone I connected with over social media. Getting straight to the point, I said, "I have a product that can help you. Give me a shipping address and I'll have it out to you by tomorrow." He responded and we spoke about me coming down to where he was to do a video as well. I don't know if I'm I or if it's the industry but I jumped on a plane ready to do business. I was prepared. This was a business trip and I always come straight when I deal. I arrived at 2 am and got a text saying, "What you wearing? I think you should come by." I never told him I was interested or that I wanted anything more than a business relationship. But that flight took off from the business runway into his fantasy world. It was one of the moments that made me feel like I didn't fit or belong in this industry. Instead of being upset though, I turned that trip into an opportunity to take some business photos and support a friend's grand opening by making a guest appearance. Like I said before, even when plans go left you have to know how to flip a situation to your advantage.

As women business leaders, we tend to get objectified. I've never crossed the line with anyone I've worked with but it says something that I even have to put that out there. My reputation in the community is solid and took a while to build, but people who deal with me know that I'll pay them their worth and I'm a flexible person to work with. People also know me for being straight with my business deals. They know that if I'm going to pay them, I better be getting something back on that investment. Whenever I'm getting ready to go to a meeting, I already have my pay scale, my timelines and my details worked out. There is never any doubt about my expectations.

I'm not about to waste my time trying to get you to see me as a business leader. If you don't, it's your loss. As a woman, you can fight to be treated the way you deserve, but don't waste time trying to connect to that one misogynistic person who refuses to see you as a business equal. While you're spending time trying to change his mind, other opportunities are passing you by. Your time is money, and the more time you spend trying to change that one mind is the more money you're not making. Look at it this way, if you're meant to work with that individual, you will. Maybe the next time, he'll be knocking on your door. Trust the process and the doors that God shuts in your face. They are being closed for a reason.

All this said, though, I love being a Black female business owner right now. It's such a great time to be a Black woman. More and more of us are opening businesses. According to a 2015 Black Enterprise article, Black women are the fastest growing group of entrepreneurs in the United States—increasing by 322 percent since 1997. Black women are also being celebrated more. In 2018, I participated in an Essence event for women entrepreneurs, where I spoke about my experience with building my business. Black women are also supporting each other more. Thanks to social media, we're connecting with other women leaders. This network allows us to share our stories and build our resilience and strength. There's something really special about women empowering other women.

All these blessings are because He first empowered me to step out of the life I knew and chase the life I wanted. God opened the door and challenged me to step through, letting me know He would be there throughout the process and would speak to me, as long as I listened. He also sent me a support system so intense that I could feel His presence through it.

## #PrayThroughTheProcess

You pray for something and God makes it so much bigger every time. He gives you an opportunity that's much greater than you initially pictured it would be. I always say, #PrayThroughTheProcess but it's more than just a saying, it's a lifestyle. You cannot get to the next level unless you incorporate

God. Thank God for giving you the good and the bad. Praying through the process is my way of thanking God but also recognizing the part He plays in my journey. When I'm in doubt or in need, I call on God. I trust that He is listening and will provide solutions to the questions I'm facing that day. When I call on God, He always answers. He reminds me I am enough.

The more you trust God, the more opportunity He has to move you to the next level.

So, I want to challenge you. When you're facing a crisis or are questioning what to do next, take a moment and pray. Ask God to guide you and help you along your entire journey. Listen with an open heart and you'll hear His response.

Let's practice a little.

*I am grateful for:*

*I could use some clarity around:*

*Right now, God, I could use your help with:*

# Chapter 3
## WHAT DREAMS ARE MADE OF

Dreams have power. They show us the path our hearts want to take. They don't care if that path is easy or not. We often look at dreams and don't think they're realistic or achievable. But the way I see it, dreams were put in us for a reason. Dreams are when we connect with God, without any barriers, as He shows us our path. It took me a while to understand the dreams He had for me because they were so different from what I had pictured in my head growing up. I didn't see myself as an entrepreneur. I didn't understand how my passion would lead to developing a revolutionary product. I never imagined writing a book or creating a tour, but meeting so many aspiring entrepreneurs who need support made me determined to give back. Our dreams take us through paths we have never seen before and down roads we would never have believed we could walk.

I wanted to share this part of my story with you because it's way too simple to just see the Jesseca who is here, without considering the path I walked to get here. I didn't always have things figured out. Just because I had a dream didn't mean I knew my way and always walked it. I used to pray all the time, asking God for His guidance and help. But I didn't see a better place, an end to my situation, and I felt stuck. We see celebrities and think that most of them were born knowing some sort of secret to success or with a silver spoon in their mouth. We don't see ourselves in these people. The most important thing I want you to know is that it is someone just like you who created a successful business, someone just like you who decided to trust God and create a powerful online platform. If I can do it, so can you.

## USING PASSION AS A COMPASS

Sometimes, I struggle with fully accepting the responsibility He gave me. On those days, I try to put my faith in God and my trust in my passion. My passion has lit my way so far, and I have to keep believing it will continue to do so. I'm not saying your passion won't change and evolve, but you have to trust that evolution.

When, as a kid, I wanted to do hair, it was that simple. Hair. That's it. As I fulfilled that dream, other goals began to appear — creating a hair product to help people, becoming an influencer and sharing my knowledge with others. Now, new passions are leading me to different and exciting opportunities. As a single mother with three kids, it would have been easy for me to accept what I had. However, being a mother also made me want to push harder to provide more for my kids and to show them they can achieve anything.

All the smart people in your life will tell you to have a Plan B ready. You know, just in case. They will tell you the statistics about how many small U.S. businesses fail (about 20 percent in their first year and 50 percent in their fifth year, if you were wondering). They will tell you how you should be rational when chasing your dream. All valid points but let's get something clear: Dreams aren't rational. They're your driven purpose, and whether they will work depends on how much faith and work you put into them.

None of this is to say you shouldn't do research because you absolutely should. You need to make sure:

1) people want your product
2) you understand the value of your product in the market

Being an entrepreneur isn't for the lazy or the faint of heart.

I never had a Plan B and I don't believe in them. I was going to make my Plan A work. It may have required some finessing and reworking but Plan A was it. Since I had no Plan B, there was no room for doubt to sneak in or for me to say, "Oh well, if this doesn't work, I can always do XYZ." Even if things ever felt like they were falling apart, I kept pushing my Plan A because there was nothing else for me. I had to make it work. I didn't always know how I would do it, but I knew I would pull through.

One of the first things you want to do is put your dreams on paper. Write them down, create a vision board or find some way other way to help make them real. For example, when you create a vision board, you're creating a visual representation of your dreams. Whenever you feel in doubt, you just need to look at the board's photos to remind you of what you're working towards. The connection you make with your vision board will help you feel connected to your dream.

## CREATING A VISION BOARD 101

Vision boards can be a mix of photos, quotes and affirmations. The components just have to be visual.

## STEP 1: IDENTIFY YOUR VISION

- Before you begin, think or pray about what you'd like to achieve. What kind of goals do you want to be reminded of daily?

- Here are some questions and statements to get you started:

    o   What does my dream home look like?
    o   How many sales do I want to make this year?
    o   I would love to be interviewed by... (Oprah, Ellen, etc.)
    o   My bank account will have XX dollars in it

- These are just some suggestions and, of course, you can create your own. Think about your personal life, your family, your work and your business.

- Dream big.

## STEP 2: GATHER YOUR MATERIALS

- You can use anything visual to put together your vision board:
    o   Images and inspirational quotes from Instagram
    o   Bible quotes
    o   Images from magazines

o   Photographs you've taken

- Glue your selected images to a poster board.

## STEP 3: CREATE SPACE FOR IT

Put the vision board up somewhere you'll see it daily (like your bedroom wall). The more you see it, the more the vision board will help you focus.

## STEP 4: HAVE FAITH

- Now that you've created your board and placed it prominently in your house, keep looking at it. Continue to work on your passion and let the vision board inspire and assist you. Be ready to take on any opportunity that comes your way.

## IDENTIFYING YOUR PASSION

Everyone's passion is different so it will take different forms. Sometimes, it's working behind-the-scenes, and other times, it's being the face of a brand. Since passions evolve as you grow, achieving what you dreamed of as a child may just be the first step in a larger journey. It may be giving you the foundation to explore another passion. If you're open to the idea that as you grow so do the things you dream about, you'll never find yourself bored or stuck. Every day is a new opportunity to build a new business and reach another level of success. If you're hesitant though, your potential clients will be as well.

I want you to consider something: What brands do you buy from? What attracts you to them? What drew you to me? The answer is usually passion, confidence and product quality. Before you tried Miracle Drops, I had you believing with The Edge Police. I got you to try it because I believed, and still do, with no doubt, that this is the best product out there. No doubt in my mind means no hesitation in my sales pitch. As a result, you believe in my product and in me.

When you unlock your passion, it won't let you sleep. And I don't mean just when you're setting up your business. I still generally work the majority of the day. I'm always filming, finding my next influencer to feature or testing my latest idea. That most likely will not change until I walk away from Kaleidoscope.

This activity is a reflection exercise that will help you make the most of each day.

- Take stock of your skills and abilities. Is there something that you're really amazing at or even slightly better at than the average person?

- If you could learn anything or improve your skills at something, what would it be?

- Track some moments when you felt completely happy and content with your life:

  o   What were you doing at that time?
  o   Who were you with?
  o   What part of that moment brought you joy?

- Track moments when you really hated your day:
  o What were you doing?
  o Who were you with?
  o What made you feel so bad?

- Track your day-to-day activities for a couple of weeks:

  o On what are you spending most of your time? Is it cooking, writing, dancing, working out, watching YouTube videos?

- What would make each day a little easier for you?

Write down every crazy idea and thought. Review your notes every night, and see if you can pick out patterns or ideas that seem interesting and worth exploring. A little-known fact about me is that I carry a notebook with me everywhere. I jot down ideas, thoughts, ways I can improve my business, and potential collabs or opportunities. I often go back and review my notebooks. I may not implement everything I've written down right then and there, but the ideas are there. Who knows where a jot in your book can take you.

## MOTIVATED AND MOBILIZED

On this entrepreneurial journey, the further you go the more distractions, hurdles and challenges you'll encounter. Often, these things feel like they are taking you away from the vision of who you want to be. The truth is, the lessons from these distractions and hurdles are also preparing and molding you to become the person you want to be in the future. Among the most basic but important things you'll need to do to become a successful entrepreneur are: remain motivated despite challenges and always be ready to act.

The way you approach your business is very much determined by what you believe about yourself and money, and your faith in your ability to sell. Let's be straight, being an influencer is about your hustle, your capacity to market your idea, your creativity and your product. If you don't have the motivation or aren't willing to learn it, you're going nowhere fast.

### Do Your Research

Something that really bothers me is when people ask me what they should do. It actually drives me crazy. I can tell you how to grow your idea, but I can't tell you what your idea is. This has to be your passion project 'cause, trust me, if you don't love it, you won't stick to it. When you're meeting any potential investor or mentor, including me, you want to show the best version of yourself. Come in prepared and ready to ask questions. It's your chance to showcase and pitch your business and to get real advice on how to build and brand the company. When I say do research and be prepared, I'm not saying you need to know everyone in your sector and write a 10-page report on each one. But you gotta show the demand for what you're trying to sell. Whether people actually want your product is the most basic fact you should know. You're about to devote all your time and energy to something; you owe it to yourself to find out if people will be willing to pay.

As Kaleidoscope grows and expands, the product is always the first thing we consider. What are we bringing to market? Who else does it? Do we have enough customers who want the product? We look at what the stores are selling then we talk to them and ask what items are moving, what issues people are complaining about and what people would like. At the start, I didn't do this. When I look back, I can see the opportunities I missed so I always tell the people I mentor, "Don't do what I did; be better." Take the lessons I'm giving you and start a few steps ahead of where I began my journey.

Thanks to social media and the internet, right now you can sell anything. Like too many late-night online shoppers will attest, we really are moving into an age where you can get anything on the internet. What you need to figure out is what percent of that market is yours. Is it, for example, three percent of the local community or 10 percent of the American market? How much of the market are you looking to claim? Also, understand who is your target client. Is your product only geared towards men, who make up nearly 50 percent of the U.S. population? Is it men between the ages of 15 and 19, which is now only seven percent of the U.S. male population? What is the best way to connect with this audience? Are members of this audience on social media? Which platforms? Is the product a one-time buy or will customers need to purchase this product continually? Is the product a seasonal item for which marketing will depend on the time of year?

Essentially, your task here is to find out:

1. Who is your demographic?
2. What are the buying patterns associated with your product?

Knowing what kind of product you have, who will be interested in buying it and how you can market to that particular group will also help you identify potential weaknesses and risks associated with your business. For example, what are you doing during the off-selling periods? How can you minimize the off-selling periods?

Here's a simple chart to help you start.

| My Product Idea | What It Does | Who It Helps | Who Else It Can Help |
|---|---|---|---|
| *What is the idea for your new product?* | *How does it serve a need in society and/or help people?* | *Who are the main users (primary target market) of this product?* | *Who else (secondary target market) could be interested in this product?* |
| E.g. Miracle Drops | - Boosts confidence<br>- Increases hair growth<br>- Helps people who have hair loss issues | - Men and women<br>- African Americans<br>- People who wear weaves and wigs<br>- People with hair loss issues | - Men and women from other communities who also experience hair loss |

## ESTABLISH YOUR PRICE POINT

Setting a price for skill set is always hard for new entrepreneurs. I struggled with it too. When it's a product, in some ways it's easier. That's because it can be more straightforward since you start with a base cost, which is the actual cost of making the product plus the shipping and packaging fee. Once you add a percentage for profit, which should include reinvestment in your company, you'll have a pretty good estimate.

| Cost of product production | + | Packing and shipping costs | + | Profit (20%) | = | Estimated price of product |

When it comes to charging for knowledge and skills, however, people tend to struggle. We're trying to price our value when, a lot of the time, we haven't made peace with how we feel about money. Money is one of those strange things people have a love-hate relationship with. We would love to have it, but we hate being tied to it. If you want to drive your business, however, you've got to drive your sales.

For $950, I'll meet with you for business consulting. I decided to provide the service, which is available through iluvcolors.com, because people kept asking me for advice and help with their businesses. That price is grounded in the idea that in helping you for an hour and offering you my expertise, I am pulled away from my business and not making sales. What is the opportunity cost that's lost to Kaleidoscope?

If I were only considering the amount of money the business makes hourly, the price would be somewhere upwards of $2,500 per hour. If you can afford that, you probably don't need any business consulting from me.

Money, as helpful as it is in achieving goals, isn't the most important thing nor is it my only motivation. I get more excited about the possibility of helping others, and draw strength from the community of women, entrepreneurs and brave people I've met through my journey. I think about them and myself when I was starting out. What was important to me? What would I have paid for? What could I afford? So, my consulting price also considers what the people I want to help can afford and the amount they would pay—which is high enough to encourage them to take our meeting seriously but low enough for them to be willing to invest in the service. Finally, you must consider what you're offering for the price you're charging. Are you providing services for which you would pay that cost? When I started out, I would have paid $950 to speak to someone about my business and get some much-needed advice.

The service you're asking people to pay for should reflect what you can do. Don't tell me you're charging $300 for social media consulting if you only have 100 followers. Make sure your business and your products are airtight and reflect your abilities. If you're offering styling skills, for example, your website and social media should be filled with different clients and various styles. A page full of selfies only shows me you can do your own hair but doesn't tell me you can recreate those styles on other people. Set up your credibility before you set up your entrepreneurial career. Social media and the internet make it very easy to check up on people's claims.

## MANAGING YOUR MINDSET

I always turn a negative into a positive. Sometimes, this works against me as I don't always deal with issues but rather bottle them up in an attempt to move forward. When I was a teen and my mom kicked me out, I did just that 'cause I didn't want anything holding me back. I don't know if I actually dealt with the emotions of the 17-year-old girl who felt like she had lost all her support. Looking at it today, I see the way holding onto the resentment affected me. I'm far more aware of how my personality traits affect my well-being and my business.

You must always maintain the mindset of a successful entrepreneur. The person you want to be in the future needs to inform the choices of the person you are right now. See that future person as a success who knows what his or her brand is worth. Creating a viral video or getting that big client is something that happens regularly for that future self. Your future self isn't limited to thinking, "Oh, this is just a hobby", "I am just starting out", "I am not that good". These kinds of thoughts are going to hurt you and you need to be aware of them. My question is, if you're not creating a business to be successful then what are you doing giving up sleep, investing time and money, taking on stress, and sacrificing time with family and friends? You may as well stay where you are, at your nine-to-five.

As you grow and adopt a CEO mindset, you'll realize the one-woman, one-man show can't last forever. You need a team you can trust. For example, expanding your business is great, but the right things must be in place for expansion so you can be ready for it. You can't handle everything by yourself and you need to be wise in choosing who you employ. Also, with expansion, it's essential to have the proper paperwork in place. You don't want to be in a position where someone can come after your work and say it's theirs. You gotta take your business seriously from day one. Even when friends offer to help with your first video, for example, make sure you're clear about who owns what parts of it and how the creative content is going to be credited. It's easy to downplay the success of your company but in today's age of viral videos and content, you always want to be prepared as if your next video will be a viral hit. Keeping the lines straight and expectations clear with friends and other collaborators will prevent anything from falling back on you.

# Chapter 4

## BLESSINGS HAVE REQUIREMENTS

Being an entrepreneur is one of the most stressful jobs you could ever have. Actually, it isn't even a job but a way of life. There are days when you'll be struggling to stay positive and days when you'll just want to quit. It's gonna be hard enough battling yourself, you don't want to be battling anyone who isn't committed to your success.

Let me put it to y'all another way. One day, you get an opportunity to invest your savings into your dream business. So, you take your startup money and get ready to make the investment. You know there is still a lot of work to do but in your heart you're certain this is the right step. You also recognize the decision comes with a lot of work but you're ready for it. As you're about to take this step, the first thing you need to do is mind your circle. Your circle should be made up of people who support you rather than those who put more barriers in your path.

Remember, not everyone is meant to receive the blessings you're receiving. God will hold back those blessings until the people you're meant to receive them with are around you. That's why it's so important to be mindful of who is already in your circle, be aware of whom you let in, and carefully think about whom you are seeking advice from. Be on the lookout for those who aren't meant to receive your blessings because they don't appreciate them and will always be ready to pull you down.

You're on the verge of investing when someone in your circle questions if this is the smartest way to spend your money. Now you find yourself not only putting energy into building your business but also trying to convince your friend that it will work. In moments like this, you'll realize there are two types of people you'll encounter throughout your life. And the difference between them is intention.

The first kind, the negative friends, don't want you to succeed. These are the people who will knock down every idea, tell you it sucks and then list all the reasons it won't work. These people don't necessarily have ill towards you, but they can't picture your success because they can't see their own vision and blessings, or their own ideas have failed. Sometimes, these people are also so damn afraid that they let their fear get in their way and yours.

The other kind is the friends who question you to keep you on the right path. The Lord brought these people into your life to help you achieve your goals. When they ask you questions, they have seriously thought through any opportunity that might come your way. They're not asking questions because they want you to say "no". They are encouraging you to consider how the opportunity will affect your brand and your clients. They're helping you find solutions so you can move ahead instead of staying where you are. These people understand success takes hard work and sacrifice. Usually, they're guided by their own vision and purpose. You're not going to have to explain your vision to them over and over because they trust in it and understand the power of taking chances and having faith. These are the people who know that a requirement of receiving God's blessings is guiding others on their path.

Blessings don't come for free. They require hard work, sacrifice and good intentions. People always say they're ready to receive a blessing but they don't think about how to be a blessing. What are you willing to sacrifice? How much are you willing to invest to receive your blessing? Can you set aside time to create a business plan and write down goals? Will you sacrifice dinner with your family or nights out with your friends? How about sleep? There are absolutely no shortcuts to creating a successful business. You must be willing to put in the work and have faith.

## YOU ARE YOUR FIRST INVESTOR

Launching any product or venture requires investment, which starts with you investing in you. I invested in my vision by putting my savings in it, and while that's important, investing is about more than money. So, capital definitely wasn't the only investment I made when I was growing my business.

Investment is about building your knowledge and skills as a leader and an entrepreneur. Investment is about dedicating time and effort. Investment is about branding yourself. When you consider the type of investments you'll need to make, ask yourself these questions:

- What type of learner am I?
- What skills do I need to succeed?
- What talents do I have that will benefit from some coaching?

When you identify the skills you need to run a successful business, see where and how you can learn them. It may be from books, classes or a mentor. Choose the method that will keep you most engaged. If you're unsure of your learning style, there are some great online tests you can complete that will help you identify it.

I always knew I wasn't much of a reader. I'm more of a hands-on and auditory learner. Basically, that means I learn best when I'm trying or doing something new, or when I talk to others about my idea or hear their insight. Knowing this, when I started, I chose to take a few classes. I realized if I wanted to advance my business to the next level and get our products out there, I would have to do some marketing. So, I signed up for a marketing course with Ming Lee, owner and CEO of the Snob Life brand. A lot of the content was familiar to me and served as a great refresher that always left me motivated. During one discussion, Ming Lee said that even though she had gotten into the hair game, she had never enjoyed doing hair and retired three years. That really stood out.

It was an ah-ha—or more like a "what the hell?"—moment for me. I had been doing hair since I was 12, and here was someone who did hair for three years and had built a successful career. It made me question what I was doing. This is also where having the right people around you comes in. While the people around me also did hair, they hadn't seen a different life for themselves, so I hadn't seen a different life for myself. We were like the blind leading the blind since none of us saw anything beyond what we were already doing. Taking Ming Lee's course opened my eyes to all the opportunities I was missing out on and made me realize I wanted to go harder. Even back then, I was big on content creation and, to be honest, she was the only other person who was doing it. Her content was movie theater quality; it was so risky, so unique and so inspirational. I knew I would learn more from her than I could on my own.

When you first start, you really don't know anything. You may have a great idea and some vague comprehension about how to bring it to the market, but you likely don't know many essential parts of the business. You may not know something as simple as pricing, creating a business plan or managing logistics. That's why it's so essential to invest in learning tools, whether it's books, YouTube videos, classes, networking or other industry events, or finding a mentor. One of the greatest things about being alive today is the internet. Starting with a simple online search will help you to begin to develop your idea.

But learning goes well beyond just taking in all the knowledge you can when you're a novice. Here's a truth you need to hear: You must always be okay with learning, no matter how far you get. No one on this Earth knows everything. Also, what you learn today may not be relevant in a couple years because nothing stays the same. You must be willing to keep up with the changes.

I am where I am because I took the time to invest back in myself. I used SMART goals (I'll explain what that is in a second), I made plans and I budgeted. For example, in terms of budgeting, I looked at my spending and identified opportunities where I could save. I then invested those savings into business essentials such as hiring a photographer and wardrobe styling. Do you need the $5-coffee from Starbucks or can you sacrifice it to save for some professional services for your brand? Be smart with what you're paying for and when you're paying for it.

When I realized that the majority of my business came from my Instagram, I invested in hiring a stylist and a makeup artist who made sure I always presented a fresh look and face. I also learned my angles and figured out my poses. If you're uncomfortable speaking to a camera, invest in speaking or acting classes. To become more confident, you can also do things at home. Take your phone, flip the camera so you can see yourself, prop it on something and then record yourself talking. Pay attention to your angles, your hand movements and your ability to articulate. Watch the video you recorded and see how you can improve. Once you've mastered this, it should be a bit easier to speak in front of a camera or people. If you're trying to make a video to post, please be hair and face ready. Investing in yourself is about presenting the best version of you to clients, sponsors and collaborators, whether on video or in person.

Presenting your best self also includes your circle. Your circle can move you forward and will contribute to your future, so that's more reason to pay attention to who you let in. Be as deliberate with your circle as you are about taking classes and reading books. Your circle should always support and inspire you, so invest energy into attracting people who motivate you rather than those who drain your energy.

## SETTING GOALS

Remember those SMART goals I mentioned above? Begin by making sure every goal you set is SMART: Specific, Measurable, Achievable, Realistic and Time-based. I also add an R (for Results) to the SMART goal setting system. I think it's always important to know why you're working towards a goal. Especially in the early days, when your resources (think funds and time) are limited, you want to invest in goals that will provide the most growth for your brand. The SMART-R system helps you to understand the actions that will support you in achieving your goals.

Here is a further breakdown of the SMART-R system.

- Specific: The goal is clearly defined.
- Measurable: How will this goal help to measure the impact of your brand?
- Achievable: What steps do you need to take to make this goal happen?
- Realistic: Can you achieve your goal with the resources you have available?
- Time-based: By when do you want to achieve the goal?

Results: What does achieving this goal mean for your brand?

There are other variations of the SMART system, but I believe this is the most effective one for growing your business. The SMART-R system will help keep you on track and prioritize the investments you're making in your brand and in yourself. When you're creating your goals, keep a couple things in mind. First, establishing a broad goal such as, "I want to grow my social media" won't help you plan to achieve the goal. Also, creating pie in the sky goals such as, "I want two million followers in six months" can be very discouraging because that isn't realistic unless you have a lot of time, money and celebrity collaborations. I'm not telling you to think small. Your goal shouldn't be to get 10 followers, who just might happen to be your family, but there is a happy medium between 10 and two million.

Let's review the SMART-R goal setting system in a bit more depth.

- **SPECIFIC:** Your goal setting process should be very focused. Instead of a general goal for your company or brand, look at particular issues you'd like to address. Do you want to increase sales? Are you looking for more social media engagement? Do you want to get involved in philanthropy in the community? Looking at specific areas of your brand and business will help you determine where you want to make a change.

- **MEASURABLE:** A lot of people tend to get stuck on this step. You need to understand the benefit of your goal by measuring its impact. If you decide to focus on increasing sales, for example, you want to include a percentage in your goal setting. Measuring your goal gives you something to check it against. If you surpass your goal, great. If you don't, you can look at the methods you tried and identify areas in which you may need to make a more significant investment, either personally or in the business.

- **ACHIEVABLE:** How are you going to execute the goal? What steps will you take to reach the goal? Do you have everything you need to take these steps? If your goal is to increase sales by connecting with other brands, how are you going to make those connections? Do you know the brands that would be interested in working with you?

- **REALISTIC:** Making a goal to work with Beyoncé when you're starting isn't realistic unless you know her personally (in which case, can I get an introduction?). As a new business owner, your time, money and resources will be limited, so if you're targeting specific brands to work with, make sure they are brands you can access with your limitations. You don't want to invest into a goal that isn't realistic.

- **TIME-BASED:** I cannot stress enough how vital it is to put yourself on a schedule. It motivates you to start working on your goal and gives you a timeline in which to reassess. If you don't give a goal a due date, it tends to drag on. You'll also find it easy to say, "Oh, I'll achieve this goal someday." "Someday" is just another excuse to not actively pursue your dreams.

- **RESULTS:** This is an especially important one. Every goal you create and devote time and money to should be moving you, your brand and your business forward. If your goal isn't doing that then reassess it! I also want you to understand the impact of your goal 'cause, right now, I know you probably have a lot of goals.

Remember, you are one person so getting all your goals done simultaneously is going to be impossible. Consider which goals will benefit your business the most and place you in a better position to go after your remaining goals.

If you put everything I just discussed together, your goal should change from:

"I want to increase my sales."

to

*"By the end of 2019 (Time), I will increase my online sales (Specific) by 10 percent (Measurable) through collaborations with other brands (Achievable) that I have a relationship with (Realistic). A 10 percent increase in sales will grow my company's profits and further develop my brand's relationship with other influencers, increasing visits to my page (Results)."*

What's critical to remember and examine about goal setting and any investment you make is the outcome. Did you achieve your goal? Why or why not? What worked? What didn't work? What can you do better? This set of questions is going to be a staple. I ask myself these questions during and after all my marketing campaigns.

Here are a few standard goals for any brand or business that's starting up. Take the time to think about and work through them using the SMART-R process.

- Develop a business plan
- Launch a social media channel
- Increase social media followers
- Create new or improved social media content
- Grow clientele
- Improve client engagement and satisfaction
- Find investors

Let's try out one of your goals below.

Goal: _____

| S | How will you make it specific? |
|---|---|
| M | How will you measure it? |
| A | What's your plan to achieve the goal? |
| R | Is the goal realistic? |
| T | Does the goal have an end date? |
| R | What was the impact of your goal on your business? |

Goals and action plans go hand in hand. Once you set your SMART-R goal, you'll need to consider how you're going to execute it. Build an action plan, which will allow you to determine where you're investing and what that investment will do for your business. The action plan doesn't need to be complicated. It can be as simple as taking a course or setting aside 30 minutes a day to email influencers. Your action plan is how you'll move your business forward.

To meet your top goal, commit to an action plan below:

_____

_____

_____

_____

_____

_____

_____

_____

## ENTREPRENEUR MUST-HAVES

I'm often asked the secret mix of ingredients to becoming a successful entrepreneur. These are the skills I think business owners need for their venture to succeed. I'll talk about them in greater detail throughout this chapter.

- **Patience:** Leveling up in your blessings takes time and sacrifice. Be patient, network, create and keep pushing towards your vision. Show God you have faith in your vision and the patience and dedication to reach it. The Lord sends small blessings, and you must appreciate and maximize them to show Him you're ready to receive bigger blessings.

- **Creativity:** I live in my head. Kaleidoscope gives me the chance to share that inner world with people. Think about the people who make an impact and stand out, like Beyoncé and Oprah. We remember them 'cause they are originals. They aren't afraid to show us who they are and they do it in a way that hasn't been done before. With my social media, nothing I do is a copy of someone else. It all comes entirely from my imagination, so it becomes uniquely Jesseca Dupart.

- **Prayer:** As you know, prayer is at the heart of everything I do. Praying through the process isn't simply a slogan on a shirt, it's part of my everyday business planning and strategy. I seek clarity for my goals and also thank the Lord for the many blessings He has provided to me. Whether you're in doubt about where your vision is taking you or celebrating your first win, pray for His guidance and express gratitude.

- **Leadership:** As a leader, you see the vision, identify opportunities and guide your team towards them. Leaders also know when to seek out and form alliances with key people who will help to expand their business. Being a strong leader allows you to connect with people who bring something new or something that you don't have to the table. Instead of being insecure, leaders create deals and generate greater value.

## SETTING UP YOUR BUSINESS

Before you go any further, you must set up your business according to the legal processes of your state or county. This includes: figuring out the type of business your company is, getting your articles of organization or articles of incorporation (which one will depend on the type of business you own), registering your trademarks and ensuring you are protected as a business.

**Evaluate and develop your business idea**
- Does this idea work for you?
- Will it make you money?
- Do you have a business plan?

**Business structure of your company**
- Are you the only owner or do you have partners?
- What is the ownership style of your business? (e.g. board of directors)

- Do you have the appropriate insurance in place? What is the coverage you need?
- How much personal liabilities coverage do you need?

## Name your business
- Think of 10 potential business names.
- Check online to see if there are other businesses with those names or similar names.
- Once you narrow down your name choices, find out if the domain name is available as a "dot com". Though you can use other endings (such as dot org), which are known as top level domains, dot com is the simplest and most used.
- Check with your County Clerk's office for any concerns with your proposed name. Is it on the list of fictitious or assumed business names in your county?
- Check with your Secretary of State to see if your proposed name is available as a corporation or a limited liability company (LLC).
- Run a federal or state trademark search for proposed names. You want to make sure your chosen name isn't famous because of another brand.

## Register your business
- Register your business in your chosen state.
- Register your business name as a federal or state trademark.
- File a trademark application.
- Register your business domain name. There are web hosting and development platforms (think Wix, GoDaddy, Squarespace and others) that can help

facilitate this. Do some research to find the platform that works best for you and can help address any concerns you have.

## Legal paperwork

- Have in place the legal paperwork for any partnerships.
- What is your ownership structure?
- Sole proprietorship
- General or limited partnership
- Limited liability company (LLC)
- C corporation
- S corporation
- Nonprofit corporation

Below is an outline of each business model. Make sure you think about and do further research into the one that will work best for you.

| TYPE | DEFINITION |
|---|---|
| **Sole proprietorship** | - One person runs the business and assumes all liability and responsibility (this will apply to most of you reading this book)<br>- Register as a local business |
| **General partnership** | - Two or more partners start the business together<br>- Usually, you just need a verbal agreement<br>- Register as a local business |
| **Limited partnership** | - You have partners who invest in your company but don't run it<br>- You need a legal partnership agreement to make sure all parties are aware of their rights and responsibilities as partners<br>- Register as a local business but also need a Certificate of Limited Partnership with the State |
| **Limited liability corporation (LLC)** | - Is a mix of corporation and partnership models<br>- Offers owners protection from being personally liable for debts amassed from the business<br><br>- Includes an LLC agreement that outlines the percentage of ownership by all members (stakeholders), |

| | |
|---|---|
| | member rights and responsibilities, and information on the use of profits<br>- Can be a single-member LLC<br>- Register as a local business<br>- Must file articles of organization (this name may vary depending on what state you reside in) |
| **C corporation** | - Is a business owned by shareholders<br>- The company — not shareholders — holds financial and legal liability<br>- Both the company and shareholders are taxed<br>- Requires greater paperwork, and you should most likely hire a lawyer<br>- Good for companies that would like to go public (become publicly traded and owned) in the future<br>- Paperwork required in most states:<br><br>• File articles of incorporation<br>• Create bylaws or rules of operation for the corporation<br>• Appoint a board of directors<br>• Issue stock certificates to initial shareholders<br>• If your business is in various locations, appoint a registered agent to receive any documents on behalf of your business. This is like the legal headquarters for your business. |

| | |
|---|---|
| **S corporation** | - Similar to a C corporation with difference in taxation model (the business is not taxed but shareholders are)<br>- Requires greater paperwork, and you should most likely hire a lawyer<br>- Good for companies that would like to go public (become publicly traded and owned) in the future<br>- Paperwork required in most states:<br><br>• File articles of incorporation<br>• Create bylaws or rules of operation for the corporation<br>• Appoint a board of directors<br>• Issue stock certificates to initial shareholders<br>• If your business is in various locations, appoint a registered agent to receive any documents on behalf of your business. This is like the legal headquarters for your business. |

I would recommend seeking the advice of a lawyer for any of these options, but especially if you go with the limited partnership, LLC, or C or S corporation models. Make sure you fully understand each model and the benefits for your business.

# Chapter 5

## FROM HAIR TO THERE

Change is inevitable. Whether it comes to relationships or business situations, everything grows and evolves. If it didn't, you'd be stagnant and that's one thing you never want to be. However, no matter how much your vision, and as a result, your brand, grows and changes, the core of it should remain who you are. This is brand identity. We'll focus a lot on this throughout this chapter.

Your brand's identity doesn't change regardless of what changes happen in your life or to your products. It's the core of you who are, as a person and business owner, and what comes to mind when people think of your company. When you're considering your brand identity, make sure it reflects you (and the future you) rather than the negative voices in your head or other people. You need to project the person you are and want to be. I know some of you will think you're not ready, smart, talented, pretty and whatever else you're letting hold you back from moving forward. Well, faith it till you make it. Be confident and show the side of you that you know is in there—the side that's ready to be CEO.

Listen to this carefully because I learned it the hard way, and I'm giving it to you here so you don't have to:

Don't let people affect the way you see yourself and don't let circumstances change the way you see yourself. You have to see yourself the way God sees you and as who you aspire to be in the future. That person isn't a fantasy, so walk like it and talk like it, even if you and your business aren't where you want to be yet. If you can think and act like that future person, it might just inspire you to take a risk and do something to move forward.

Everything you need to succeed is already in you. The future self you're envisioning is just an elevated version of you. That other person is only elevated because he or she has the confidence to go and execute the things you've been dreaming of. God has given you the vision to succeed. And He doesn't just randomly throw us visions 'cause then mine would have been to be Beyoncé! I'm just playing. I love myself and hair was always it for me; I'm just showing you that sometimes what we fantasize about isn't necessarily what we're meant to do. He gives us visions that align with who we are and the way in which we can best impact the world. You have to trust that fact and move toward it.

I often see people caught up in the idea that they don't know enough to start. Life isn't an exam. It's your classroom, and you're going to keep growing, learning and failing. You don't need to have all the answers or know exactly where you'll end up. You just need to start moving. How do you expect things to change if you're standing in the same spot? Only when you start moving will you know if the road that you're on is the one for you or if you should be turning left or pivoting right. With each step you take, you'll also realize the mountain that was looming far ahead is a hill and the deep scary looking forest is Eden.

To help you get moving, find what motivates you to get up and hustle. While some people like to believe money is a bad thing to be motivated by, there's nothing wrong with it. When I started, I wanted to make money because it brought me stability, security and the ability to take care of my own. Being financially straight is something that will help you and your business. Also, when you're secure in what you have, it's more natural to think about filling your heart.

You're a work in progress. Embrace that! If you don't yet see the full vision, trust that what you do see is part of the process taking you to a higher goal.

As you know, when I started, I wanted to do hair, own a shop and create. As my brand grew, it became about doing hair and helping people dealing with alopecia. Then I started meeting women who wanted to start businesses and didn't know how. In response, I created my U Better Get This FREE Knowledge tour to help them learn and succeed. Social media and marketing drive a large part of my brand, so Kaleidoscope Marketing became a new venture. I met new people who encouraged me to expand my business skills, which led to launching Kaleidoscope Realty. As you can see, because my vision is more limitless, I've become a business owner, entrepreneur, influencer, marketing specialist, and most recently, real estate investor and landlord. I'm not bragging, but I do want you to use my journey as motivation.

I want you to see that the Jesseca who was styling hair only saw herself as a business owner and couldn't imagine taking all these chances. However, as she grew, met new people and learned, she saw more of God's vision for her. It took a lot of investing in myself, taking some of my profit and spending it on my business and me to realize that vision. I have held checks with so many zeros behind the number that I shake my head. That money is tempting but, in those moments, you have to turn around and put it right back into the business.

We always think, "When I 'make it', I'll be okay." Firstly, you never really make it because you always have to be on your hustle, making sure you're always developing your brand and growing your business. As time passes, things change and you must upgrade your skills to continue to perfect your craft and stay on top of your game. Just like phone apps get updates, you have to update yourself. The most important part of running a business and a brand is staying current and relevant.

Secondly, success is addictive. Once you achieve something, you realize you can do more. You keep hustling and seeing another goal that you want to strive for. Every time you think you're close to you making it, you realize you just achieved a smaller goal to get you to where He wants you to be. One of the top questions I get asked in interviews or by people in general is, "What do you do for fun?" or "how do you unwind?" I work!

I'm not playing when I say work is my fun time. I'm always thinking of new ideas and opportunities. What can I try next? What's going to push me to new levels? How can I prepare for it? I know He has a plan for me and my excitement comes from discovering it. When you know you have good things coming, wouldn't you want to see what's next? It's like getting a huge gift box with a gift and a smaller box with an even better present and another box and so on. Creating businesses and building brands is the gift for me, and I can't wait to open the next box and help people open theirs.

Trusting the Lord's vision for you is a powerful and freeing feeling. When you believe in what you're doing, you begin to attract people who also believe in you and your vision. You'll be surprised by how easy it is, once you have committed to achieving success, to gather people in your corner. And these aren't just people who support you but rather people who see you as the go-to person for the problem you're trying to fix. They understand that you're going to positively impact the community.

As you start to gain traction, you'll also notice an outpouring of love and people suddenly wanting to be your best friend. Some will want to be with you 'cause they see your vision, and others will just want a piece of you. You have to get real discerning at this stage. Value quality over quantity and you'll find that it does your brand a lot more good. Your community, both on and offline, should reflect you as an individual and a brand.

The quality over quantity mantra is also important because when you develop your social media platforms, or your business in general, it's easy to fall for the numbers. Numbers are crucial but you don't want to be chasing them. You'll lose unnecessary energy wondering why people don't like your videos or posts. But, more importantly, you'll lose your brand vision. In simple terms, don't forget who you are by chasing a bunch of people who want to hang with the popular kids for a minute. Instead, provide people with value, and do so consistently, whether it's through rich content, honest truths or advice. Worry about showing people who you are, what you represent, what you stand for and why they should trust you. As you position yourself to help others, the value of what you're offering your customers increases.

## CREATING SOLID CONNECTIONS

Being an entrepreneur is about making a profit. However, one of the most critical skills of entrepreneurship is the ability to build strong relationships. Creating a community that feels a genuine connection to you and your product is vital for establishing brand loyalty. I have people who buy from me even when they have a cabinet full of Kaleidoscope Hair Products (KHP) because they want to support me. That's a loyalty built on trust and support. I consider the love the community has for me sacred and respect that it's given with an open heart.

Honoring and respecting my community's love, and by extension, the rest of the community means making sure I always put out quality products and provide excellent customer service. When people buy KHP or seek advice from the Kaleidoscope Marketing team, they're asking me to give them my honest and best advice. They know I'm not about to con them into buying a service or product that's not right for them. Their faith that I have their best interests in mind is what makes them Kaleidoscope clients.

This brand faith has translated into potential clients for Kaleidoscope Realty. Even though I bought a plaza that was fully leased out with two-year leases, I had people hitting up my social media to ask if I had room for their store. These people know that if they're part of a Kaleidoscope business venture, I'll look out for them because that's what Jesseca Dupart does. Developing a brand that's consistent, trustworthy and honorable is the best marketing tool you have. Trends, marketing ads and viral posts can all be forgotten, but a brand that speaks to who you are should always remain the core of your business.

Let's begin by thinking of 10 words that describe your brand. They can be words that are important to you (such as "faith" or "community"), words that describe you (such as "fun" and "committed") or words that describe your product (such as "quality" and "innovative").

My brand is:

1)_____

2)_____

3)_____

4)_____

5)_____

6)_____

7)_____

8)_____

9)_____

10)_____

Now, highlight your top three words. These three words are the foundation of your brand. They're the part of your brand that's reflected in everything you do, from the kind of products you sell and the influencers you connect with to all the social media captions you create. Keep these words in mind as you read on.

## GATHER YOUR IDEAS AND RESEARCH

When creating your brand, ask yourself what you want your brand to say and what problem you're trying to solve. Sometimes, the answer comes to you because it's something you do well that others want to learn. To gain some more insight, start paying attention to brands, influencers and products you currently use or follow.

Also, it's better to quietly and steadily build your brand. There's no reason to rush to have it all at once because you know your vision will eventually take you there anyway. The foundation has to be so strong that even if the house shakes, it doesn't crumble. That takes time.

Similarly, successful businesses didn't suddenly decide to do something and then announce and launch it the next week. We take our time, making sure that every detail is what we want it to be and the cost allows us to make a quality product while still turning a profit. One of the most consistent pieces of advice I give to people who seek mentoring from me is to be quietly confident. The world doesn't need to know your idea while it's in production. Keep it close to your heart as you research and develop it.

At this stage, your idea is both vulnerable and valuable. That's why people who discuss their ideas with others during the concept formulation period get discouraged. Because you haven't yet done your research to be able to defend your idea or understand if it's viable, it's easy to get sidetracked by others' comments and fears. You don't want to spend your energy defending what you want to do if you're not yet sure it's the right product. And the easiest way to prevent that is to keep quiet about it.

Instead, use the chart below to do a comparative analysis.

| What is my product*/ what does it do? | What is a comparable product on the market right now? | What do I really like about the comparable product? (price, marketing, photo quality) | How is my product unique from the comparable one? | How is my product better or how can I make my product better? |
|---|---|---|---|---|
| | | | | |

*Though I most often use the term "product" throughout the book, the same rules apply if you offer a service. In that case, your product is the service.

Research, research and research the heck out of everything. You need to fully understand the market you want to enter. Who are your competitors? What is the product demand? Who uses your product? Is it profitable for you to create this product? This last question gets a lot of people in trouble. I touched on this in Chapter 3, but it's important to reiterate in more detail because it really surprises me how few people understand how to price their product.

If I asked what you would charge for your product, I'm sure you could tell me a number. However, I am also reasonably sure that not many of you could tell me how you came up with that number or what that number takes into account.

I think of it as infomercial syndrome. We're so used to hearing $19.99 or $29.99 that we go, "Yeah, I think about $20 should cover my product". But when you factor in the average cost, shipping fees, and marketing and operating costs, the actual cost of the product may be $25. Essentially, at $20, you're losing $5 on every sale. It's not enough to look at the average cost of your product in the market. You must also consider if that production cost is realistic for you. Your competition (think big box stores) can produce your product at a lower price than you. So, you have to ask yourself how you can compete at a lower price point. Is it worth and/or profitable competing against them? How will you differentiate your product? Will it be a luxury item?

The research you conduct is also, and perhaps more importantly, going to help you understand how to position your brand differently than everyone else. Knowing and understanding your brand's value in the marketplace will help drive the growth of your business.

**Market research will help you identify:**
- what your product/brand is by recognizing potential gaps;
- the cost of creating your product/brand; and
- how to position your product/brand in the market.

## ILUVCOLORS.COM: YOUR BRAND'S IDENTITY

The brand is you. With a brand named, Kaleidoscope and an iluvcolors.com URL, you already know there's nothing dull about me. From my own hair to my video productions, Kaleidoscope Hair Products (KHP) is all about leading a fun and colorful life. It's about seizing every moment and not fading into the background when you were made to stand out.

When I opened Kaleidoscope Hair Studio, I knew it wasn't going to be your typical salon. I didn't see myself working in a shop with the black and white marble decor that many stylists love. The lack of color was uninspiring. I wanted women to feel energized and joyful when they walked into my shop. For many women, getting their hair done is the only time they can relax and walk out feeling like a million dollars. So, I focused on curating a luxurious experience in a fun environment. I chose every aspect, from the paint to the chandeliers, which I had to hunt down because I knew the details were essential. Kaleidoscope Hair Studio was a colorful extension of my personality. When you create a brand, you aren't building something fake. You have to be ready to show yourself to the world.

I think this is why people hesitate or fall off the social media wagon. There's a level of authenticity and vulnerability that's required. It's tempting to only share bite-sized and digestible parts of you. However, that's not honoring your brand or you. If you just show the world the parts of you that are "socially acceptable" and "correct", you leave out the things that make you unique. Your unique qualities help you rise and allow for a genuine connection with individuals. Being as authentic as you can in your brand also shows customers how you and your brand will respond to crises and to their concerns.

No matter where I am or what's happening around me, I stand by my Kaleidoscope community. When I feel someone has a low spirit, I pray for him or her and have a conversation with God. People also know they can talk to me when they're feeling low. It doesn't drain me to pray for them because it's part of my everyday practice, so I'm not extending my energy in a way that will tire me out. Since my connection with God and my faith is a large part and parcel of who I am, it's also a part of my brand. I could play it safe and keep church separate, but that wouldn't be genuine and I'd be withholding an essential part of myself from my community.

You also can't fake being nice or caring about people. If you're not interested in their issues or concerns when they tell you something isn't working, you won't be engaged in solving their problem and you'll default to lousy customer service.

Where you come from will also shape your brand identity. Everything about New Orleans is different, and that uniqueness is infused in every experience from dance and art to food to hairstyles. Everything about me draws from New Orleans culture. Your location will also influence your brand story in more subtle ways. For example, being in New Orleans influences how I support my community, like the bicycle program I facilitated with the New Orleans police department or supporting the city's new business owners. A while ago, I participated in #PayItForwardForNola, a campaign during which Black business owners supported small businesses. If you know my brand, my participation in that movement will come as no surprise. I believe successful people should support up-and-comers. Also, my love for New Orleans has always been evident through my Instagram posts and how I give back to the city, so a campaign that allows me to support small local businesses was a complete no-brainer. Since my brand is just me, its default practices aren't difficult to decipher because the question is always, "What would Jesseca do?"

**Your brand identity is:**
- an extension of you and your values;
- authentic in showing who you are; and
- influenced by your location.

## WHAT IS YOUR WHY?

Why do you want to be an entrepreneur? Many entrepreneurs suffer from depression, anxiety and other mental health issues. There will be days when you're ready to return to the safety of a nine-to-five. As a business owner, you're not just responsible for your livelihood but the livelihood of everyone who works for you. Needless to say, the entrepreneurial route is not an easy one. You think you understand being stressed? Wait until you start your brand.

Understanding why you want to create your brand will help keep you on track during the days you're ready to call it quits. Everyone has a different reason for wanting to become an entrepreneur. You gotta find yours.

Recognizing your motivation will also help you comprehend the risks you're willing to take for your brand and your deal breakers. When I started, financial stability was my driving force so I was very self-motivated. While my motivation has changed over time, one thing remains the same: Every month I try to beat what I accomplished the previous month. I eliminate the stuff that didn't work and perfect the things that did. Whenever I feel like slacking off, I know I'm self-sabotaging and creating an opportunity for the devil to take me off track. I'm too competitive with myself to let that happen. If one month I see my sales decrease, I get annoyed with myself but it motivates me to do better. I take steps to ensure that the next month I'm going to kill it. And that doesn't just mean doing better than that slow month, but even better than the month before that. My drive for success has kept me accountable.

Beyond being motivated by my brand's success, I wake up now wanting people to know God also has a vision for them and that when they open themselves to Him, they'll find it. My community now focuses on helping women achieve their dreams. In passing on my blessings, I remain passionate about the work I do.

We know we want to be successful but we aren't always sure why. Understanding the passion that drives us takes a lot of reflection and work. Knowing how much of a positive impact you can make to the world will keep you going when you want to throw in the towel. Daily, I get messages from women and girls telling me how much I inspire and motivate them. So, when I feel like quitting, I know I wouldn't just be quitting on me but also them, and that's unacceptable to me.

**Understanding your motivation and passion will:**
- help you push your limits and try new things;
- keep you accountable to your business;
- support you when things seem tough; and
- grow and change as you do.

## IDENTIFY YOUR TARGET MARKET

Who is going to use your product and where are they located? Why would the potential client want to use your product? Because I knew my client base had a need, expanding from owning a hair studio into Kaleidoscope Hair Products (KHP) made sense for my business growth. Doing hair for more than 20 years, I understood my clients' needs in a way not many people could, which was a direct result of always listening to their concerns. In this way, I was lucky as I could "soft pitch" ideas to my clients in conversations and see how they reacted. So, when I launched my business, it was all about taking those concerns and finding a solution for them.

In addition to listening to their hair concerns and issues, as a stylist I knew what I was looking for in products to help my clients or to create a certain look. I didn't realize it at the time, but I had been doing market research from the very first time I did hair in high school.

A product mainly fails due to two reasons: It wasn't tested on the market to see if there is a demand and the company attempting to sell the product doesn't understand its consumers and the best way to reach them.

Knowing your market will prevent that, as it will influence the products you create, help you draft the right kind of messages and elevate your business. To do so, you want to build the type of familiarity in your brand that makes them trust and connect to your product. Answering the below questions will help you to think about your target market and develop a client profile you can use to draft and create your voice and core message.

**Ask yourself:**
- Who would use my product?
- Which of their problems am I providing a solution for?
- What do they enjoy doing?
- What keeps them awake at night?
- What annoys them?
- How do they spend the day?
- How will my product fit into their day?
- What activities make them lose track of time?
- How will they use my product to improve their day?

I'm also a part of my target market. The women who use KHP are women like me. They experiment with color, weaves and styles. They enjoy life and are ambitious, with many things on the go. They're looking for something that fits easily into their lives, with little hassle. When I'm launching a product or a service, my first question is, "Would I use it?" Being a part of your target market is smart and useful because no one understands your needs better than you.

Creating a brand isn't just about an attractive design or logo but also about providing people with a platform that makes they feel like they belong to a community. Products come and go, but connecting your audience to your brand through targeted messaging ensures brand loyalty. Take Nicki Minaj and her "Barbs" or Beyoncé and the "Beehive". These people aren't just fans of the artists' music but connect to them as strong Black women who have overcome many obstacles while remaining true to their roots. Fans who belong to these communities don't only feel supported by the artists but also by their fellow fans. They feel like they're part of this super strong group of empowered women and connect to others through that network.

A quick note of caution: Like any part of developing your business, your target market is not static. As your business and brand grow and evolve, so will your target market. Consistently check so that you're aware of any changes to it. These changes can come out of people naturally "growing out" of your product or a development in the industry that makes your product less desirable to some of your clients.

To start, hair styling was my main focus and hair products were secondary. My early Instagram page showed both sides of my business. However, as KHP became more successful, I reoriented my Instagram to focus on that aspect. Eventually, I gave up doing hair entirely. Though the majority of my market stayed the same, I still watched for the possibility of new opportunities, what new products my target market wanted and how it changed. Moving away from styling to a product also meant I was now connecting to people worldwide. They no longer had to be in New Orleans to get my product (my hair styling), and I could ship KHP to them—wherever they were in the world. My target market had just blown up.

To reiterate, to build your brand identity:

- research and understand your target market;
- ask yourself who they are and why they need this product;
- find out how your product improves their lives;
- understand how powerful of a tool it is to know your market; and
- make sure you're always aware of changes to your target market.

# Chapter 6
## FROM EDGE POLICE TO INFLUENCER

The very first Instagram series I ever did was The Edge Police. I was looking for a way to talk about a serious issue, alopecia, in a way that wouldn't scare people. No one wants to talk about going bald or losing hair, and it's an awkward conversation to have. The hair loss industry, however, is a billion-dollar industry , as the condition affects more than 50 million people in the United States alone . So, what does that tell you?

It told me this was an area where I could make a change. If people were spending billions of dollars on products that weren't working, I could create something that actually did work. I knew my clients and the troubles they were having, so it made sense. The second thing these stats told me was the market was saturated and I had to stand out. A lot of people were selling everything from wigs and transplants to "cures" and pills. All of them had an expert scientist, doctor or someone else telling buyers why their product was the best. I wasn't going to get noticed by doing the exact same thing as everybody else. To put it a different way, are you going to stop at the Instagram picture that looked the same as the last 1,000 you scrolled by or are you going to stop at the one that stands out 'cause it's unique?

I let my imagination loose, took all the crazy ideas in my head and decided if I was going to do this, I'd have fun with it. I'm a joker who loves to laugh and make people happy. I played to these strengths, surrounded myself with people who would help me bring my dreams to life and shot my first episode of The Edge Police.

I understood the people in my target audience enough to know they didn't need another "expert" telling them how bad they had it or making them feel worse before offering to solve their problem. The people in my target audience also didn't need to feel like life was over and there would be no more joy until they got whatever hair recovery product a company was selling. I wanted them to have a laugh and feel good. When people feel good, they are more likely to be open to trying something different.

## TELLING YOUR BRAND STORY

New businesses usually think "brand story" refers to the company's story and end up talking about what the company does. The brand story is actually about you and highlighting the values that are important to you, especially those that underline customer care and service. It may be your brand, but the customer is at the center of it.

The brand story also has emotional reach and is the template for every communication with clients, from emails to your ads and your website. For example, my personality is about color and being playful, so the web address for Kaleidoscope Hair Products (KHP) is iluvcolors.com. Not only does my site's address reflect my personality but the layout, blog content and photos do as well. There's no confusion about what site you're browsing and my company's brand identity.

You brand narrative should include the following elements and techniques:

### The story behind the start of the business

- My come-up story is well known and that was by design. I wanted people to know where I came from so that they could see how far they could go. Whenever there's an article or piece about me or KHP, the messaging includes points such as:
  1. "Meet Jesseca Dupart, who turned her passion into a hair care empire";
  2. "gives back";
  3. "New Orleans native"; and
  4. "successful female entrepreneur".

- These are all pieces of my identity that are very important to me, and in turn very important to the brand: A female New Orleans entrepreneur who took her passion, created a successful hair care business, KHP, and gives back through her platform.

### How you provide value

- What are you doing to surprise and delight customers? Are you going above and beyond your promise to them? There are other hair products out there, but with mine you also get the full range of information on hair care.

For example, we write blog posts on seasonal hair trends, foods that help you care for your hair from the inside and company updates. Our messaging ensures our clients are always part of the Kaleidoscope family.

**Keep your story clear**
- Through my Instagram (@darealbbjudy), I can provide a lot of behind-the-scenes glimpses into my life and my company. Customers can see my thought process and some of the insanity that occurs with running a business. Since my brand reflects who I am as a person, the stories they see on @darealbbjudy are consistent with what they see in all KHP marketing. This includes the fun stuff we get up to, my colorful office decor and the projects we're working on. Even my connection with the Lord and my belief in #PrayThroughTheProcess is on my Instagram and my site. The messaging on my social media, website and in my marketing materials is consistent.

**Creativity is your friend**
- Be authentic in your brand narrative. Everyone can easily tell the story of having a passion and turning it into a business, but what's your hook? What's the creative part of your story that's unique and makes you different? Funny enough, I always think the unique part of my story is that I'm like everyone else. I didn't go to college even though I graduated high school with honors. I'm an average person who trusted the vision God gave her and was able to create something spectacular. Now I can give back to others because of it. How you tell your story will determine if others will be interested in where you and your brand are heading.

- In addition to telling your story, you have to think about how you're going to tell it. We're so lucky because today there are many exciting ways to share a brand narrative, from creating an "about me" section on your site and sharing your story in video format to creating a manifesto or, like me, using social media. Choose the one you're most comfortable with and that makes the most sense with your brand and work with that.

**Be you**
- The Lord created one of you on purpose as only your particular combination of personality, drive, outlook and passion can result in the vision He has for you. Other creators and brands can inspire you but, in the end, you are what differentiates your brand. Always honor that.

- Your brand story isn't about making a sales pitch or getting a new customer. If you sell a good product that will happen naturally. Instead, it's about connecting like-minded individuals to your brand. Potential partners will know who you are before they even meet you. It leads to authentic collaborations and partnerships with people who trust the way you believe in your brand.

- As you share and create your brand story, you may find that some people aren't interested. That's fine because your brand isn't for everyone. On the flipside, be just as discerning with the people you let in to work with your brand. You wouldn't hang out with people you don't respect or those who don't respect you or your values, so why make them a part of your brand?

**To recap, a good brand story:**
- allows you to emotionally connect with your audience;
- is the template for all messaging regarding your brand;
- must be consistent; and
- should be selective, genuine and as authentic as you.

## KNOW YOUR (MARKETING) STREAM

Thanks to social media, connecting and communicating with people has never been as easy as it is today. According to statistics, in 2018 more than 77 percent of Americans were on social media . Marketing Tech News, meanwhile, reports that the average person has seven social media accounts . Social media gives you access to a whole lot of people across the entire world. In the search to connect with the most clients, it's tempting to flood the social media market. That might make sense if you have a 50-person social media team dedicated to creating and posting content for you. But trying to successfully be on every platform on your own is not only going to drain your energy, time and passion, but it also makes no sense.

Not every social media platform makes sense for every business. Even if you were to focus on the Big 5 (Facebook, Instagram, Snapchat, Twitter and YouTube), that's still a lot of content and profiles to maintain. If your target market is 35 years and older, you're not going to find it on Snapchat. If you're trying to connect with men, starting a Pinterest account makes little to no sense since only 16 percent of registered users are men . Narrow your list of viable platforms by determining which ones your target audience utilizes most.

Once you determine what makes the most sense, start with two social media platforms you feel comfortable using, see which platform grows naturally and focus on that.

In saying that, if you create two profiles you do have to make sure you're consistently maintaining both. You can focus on one over the other, but one of the worst things for any business is appearing out of date and having irrelevant information posted on one of its accounts. Instagram, Facebook and YouTube are the platforms I use. However, I focus the majority of my attention on Instagram because it has the most followers (1.4 million across my two accounts). Of my three social media platforms, my YouTube probably has the lowest number of subscribers but I still share on it, creating and posting new content such as Judy Springer.

Beyond determining which platforms your target market uses, there are a few things to consider when choosing social media networks. Start by asking yourself whether you'll enjoy interacting on a certain platform. If you hate going on Facebook, don't choose it as your main point of engagement. You'll either start ignoring customers because you don't want to go on the platform or you'll become resentful that you have to go on it. That said, if your target audience is only on Facebook then you have to put on your grown-up pants and get a Facebook account. Find something that makes the platform enjoyable or schedule time to check in on that particular platform.

Also, look at where your competition and the brands you admire are posting and sharing. Again, you don't want to duplicate what they're doing, but you will gain some great tips, tricks and habits for how to best interact with your target audience. What hashtags are they using? How effective are their giveaways and competitions? Is this something you should consider? What would make your brand stand out if put side by side with theirs?

Although the core of your target market stays the same, people who are interested in or are buying your product or don't. How you interact with them will vary. Instagram is all about images and 60-second videos, whereas Facebook may allow greater interaction through longer posts. Also, what works for everyone else may not work for you, so keep that in mind. Because Instagram is where the majority of my audience is, I post on there when I want an opinion or an answer to a question. For example, when I went to China in 2018, I asked people on Instagram for recommendations although I know other users "check into" a place on Facebook and "seek recommendations".

The last thing I'm going to say about social media for now is: be consistent. As with your messaging, you want every platform to contain the same type of language, colors, style and tone. When I create a post, I always want the reaction to be, " That's Judy or Kaleidoscope." My videos and my Instagram posts have a very similar fun, creative and colorful feel—all words I associate with my brand. When I post a video, there is no confusion about what I'm referring to, who I am and what Kaleidoscope is.

**Knowing your marketing stream can:**
- help you find the best platform to connect with your target market;
- keep you from overextending your energy and time; and
- create consistency in your messaging.

## DON'T BE BORING. EVOLVE

You are amazing. Let's start with that truth.

Creating and building a brand and a business will take a lot of energy and faith. In starting this journey, you're inventing a different life for yourself. You're looking at your future self and thinking of what do you need to get there. You're going to be taking chances and pushing past your comfort zone.

The Edge Police, for example, was my first time trying such a bold approach. I was essentially going up to strangers to talk about hair loss. It took courage but it paid off. I was starting out and I didn't have a lot to lose. Today when I start something or create an idea, I think about it two or three times to make sure the return on the investment will be worth it. The more you have to lose, the more likely you'll be to hesitate, to change anything or to take a chance.

As an established and successful brand, it's easy to stay in your comfort zone. You know your messaging is on point and you have a loyal client base, so it seems risky and unnecessary to revisit your branding. However, nothing kills a brand more than being stagnant. Changing, evolving and reevaluating your brand are natural parts of growing your business. Even big brands such as Nike reassess who they are and what they stand behind. The "Just Do It" slogan used to refer to not making excuses and getting fit. But as Nike's target market evolved and became more socially conscious and aware, it became about surpassing limits set by society and making a change. The company took an existing idea and created something new that better reflected its evolving brand.

Your brand's core values can stay the same but how you choose to express them may become different. Today, for me, Kaleidoscope is about chasing your dreams and following the path God has set out for you. But, as you may remember, initially I saw His vision for me in the creation of hair products that would help people. That was until my business grew and became successful, and I realized that KHP was actually a means to help me get to my real mission of assisting others in chasing their dreams. My brand's identity to help people evolved from changing the way we spoke and treated alopecia to helping people achieve their goals.

If you haven't figured it out by now, self-reflection and analysis are significant and essential steps in building a brand that lasts. Be innovative, take chances and try new things. As someone who is starting out or smaller, you have more opportunity than prominent brands to create, fail, create again and succeed. Bureaucracy can hinder bigger brands. While you can take the initiative and try something entirely new and different quite easily, the ideas of bigger brands must go through a tedious approval process. Use that to your advantage.

As a new and smaller brand, you consistently have the opportunity to be a disrupter. Embrace that thinking and try all your crazy ideas. It's in those crazy ideas that the magic happens. Take every opportunity you have to create that magic rather than falling into the trap of settling into the safe and boring.

**Consistently assessing your brand is vital to ensuring that:**
- your brand is growing with your business;
- your values are in alignment with your brand; and
- you are staying fresh and relevant.

## TROLLS AND OTHER SMALL-MINDED CREATURES

As I've mentioned, creating an authentic brand and presence on social media requires a high level of vulnerability and openness. You don't have to share all of you to be vulnerable, but you do have to share your "baby", your product, which you developed and put together. There's nothing scarier than sharing something you create with the world, even if you think it's the best. You can trust that it's ready and you can pray to the Lord, but nothing will fully prepare you for putting your product out there.

Some people are looking to bring down other people. As you become more popular and your business matures, you'll see an increase in negative comments. Some people, whether or not they know you personally, don't know how to handle your success. These people will go out of their way to show you that you're just not good enough. Their energy has more to do with them and where they are in their life than with you and all your accomplishments. You won't have time to process their negativity because you'll be too busy chasing your goals.

But I'm not going to lie to you, in the beginning the messages from the trolls and others may get to you. If you must, give them five minutes of your time by taking a moment to rage, cry, vent and get angry as all heck. Then, move on because you have an empire to build. Your energy is precious and you can't waste it on anyone who drains you. More importantly, when you let trolls and those who want to bring you down take your energy, you end up losing motivation and focusing too much on their negativity.

While you may think turning off the comments on your posts will solve it, negative comments will still find their way to you.

You also want to give the positive people an opportunity to interact with you and with each other. Because someone is always going to have an opinion on what you're doing or not doing, what you're tweeting, what you're wearing and so on, you can't control what they say or type. You can, however, manage if you will listen and respond to them. That means you decide whether to leave the comments on a post, respond or delete them.

I remember watching a Tyra Banks interview where she spoke about her mom telling her it was essential to always separate "Tyra Banks the person" and "Tyra Banks the product". Her mom wanted her to understand that when casting agents were rejecting her, they were rejecting the model, not the person. Using this method, Tyra was able to build a mental wall that helped her survive modeling while keeping her sanity in check. You've got to figure out how you're going to build that kind of protective mechanism and recognize when you need to implement it.

You have to remain accountable to yourself, which means making sure you're taking care of you. Whether it's praying more, venting to your friends, keeping a motivation and/or gratitude journal or revisiting and repeating those affirmations you crafted in Chapter 1, your mental health is important. Develop a method to deal with the negative people or your mental sanity is going to be at risk.

Find a balance in what you share as well. Not everyone needs to know what you're thinking or doing all the time. You get to choose and set boundaries. Share what's needed when it's required.

I'm pretty blessed because I have built my community with positive vibes and support, so when a troll attacks my community supports me and we move past it together. The Kaleidoscope community has supported me by calling out others who steal my work or comment negatively on my posts, or even celebrities who have tried to bring me down on their personal platforms. When your fans and supporters know who you are, you'll find you won't need to waste energy on negative people because so many positive people will be uplifting you. And when you stay genuine to yourself, you won't even feel the need to respond to trolls.

When it comes to social media platforms, controls do exist for you to minimize the amount of negativity that filters through to you. Block people, filter out words that are inappropriate and report comments. Your social media is a safe space, so you don't need to feel guilty or ashamed for deleting hurtful or negative comments, or reporting someone who is trolling or bullying you. Also, don't hesitate to seek assistance from others, including the social media platform's "help" options, whenever you need to.

## CRAFTING YOUR MESSAGE

The chart below will help you craft the message for your brand. The message is just the first part. You also want to test your audience's reaction to the message and make sure it's hearing what you want to get across. So, once you're done writing, share your message with a few trusted potential clients, friends or supporters.

| Questions to Consider | Why it Matters |
|---|---|
| **Target Market** | |
| What's in it for them? | You want to show your target market the benefit of using your product. |
| What language are they comfortable with? | Use language that's geared towards members of your target market. You'll communicate differently with your clients than you will with your investors. However, you always want to make sure you're being genuine by using words that sound like you. |
| What matters to them? | What are the concerns your target audience? For example, if it's hair loss, why are they worried about losing hair? Is it the lack of confidence, not feeling sexy or other reasons? Once you understand why the problem and the solution matter, you'll know the right words to use. |
| **Your Product** | |
| What makes your product better? | What advantage does your product have over anything currently on the market? What value does it offer? |
| What makes your product different? | What are the some of the strengths of your product? |
| **Call to Action** | |
| What's next? | End with the action that you want the audience to take. Where/how can they buy your product or how they can invest with you? |

# Chapter 7

## SHY PEOPLE MAKE SHY MONEY

The first time I did The Edge Police, I was nervous as all heck. I didn't know how people would react. Forget social media—I was going up to people on the street to talk about their edges! I wasn't shy, but walking up to strangers takes another level of outgoing. I had a choice though. I could take a chance and talk to people about my product, or I could stay in the shadows and Kaleidoscope Hair Products (KHP) would never get the spotlight it deserved.

Selling a product isn't just about knowing your product is good. It's about having enough faith in yourself and in your product to sell it. You can create the best service, experience or product, but if you're not willing to put yourself on the line, there isn't going to be anybody to help you. Being shy doesn't get you very far in the world of small business. I'm not saying that you'll never be successful if you're introverted; I know many business owners who are introverted or shy. They know, however, that there's a time to step out of their comfort zone and strategically approach others. You have to put yourself in the path of opportunity for that blessing to come your way.

Success follows success. What that means is you have to show people you're successful for them to see you as a success and want to invest in or with you. One of the very first major purchases I made to reward myself was my Bentley. I got that car because I thought my opportunities would be limited unless I got others to see me in a certain light. To get bigger and better collaborations, I had to show these celebrities and business people I was playing on their level. Another example of this is the 2018 launch of Kaleidoscope Realty. I know I got this opportunity because I was connected to the right people, who saw that I could play at their level and invited me into the real estate game.

Understanding money isn't just about making sense of your running record of transactions and figuring out expenses and losses. You have to understand how money can work for you. How do you take $10 and make it $20? What's the best way to spend that $10 to get the most return on each dollar? You have to creatively examine your finances and figure out what you can do with your money today that's different from yesterday. You don't have to pursue all your ideas, but forcing yourself to seek new opportunities or smart ways to spend the money will help you come up with innovative solutions, some of which you can implement.

Figuring out how to improve your cash flow can also help you determine what structures your business is missing. In 2017, the Kaleidoscope marketing team met with Target about putting our hair products in its stores. Even though we didn't make the deal that day, the meeting made us realize we needed to revisit that goal because the structure of the business isn't ready to accommodate big box stores. Now, I look at my money and say, "Okay, how are you going to work for me so that I can get my products into Target?"

I get it, as small business owners we're never sure when our business will be self-sustaining. At the start, you budget and watch every dollar to manage risk, so what I'm about to say may sound counterintuitive: Sometimes, you'll need to take a chance with money and show it off to reap more significant blessings. For the Target deal, for example, I'd have to demonstrate that I could hold its minimum inventory requirements and be ready ASAP to fill any orders while maintaining my online stock and commitments to other retailers. A big box store doesn't want to worry about not having a product for its customers, so I'll have to invest in showing that we're financially able to meet its order requests.

When it comes to anything finance related, make sure you're considering every aspect of your business and understanding the risks.

## THE SUCCESSFUL, SOW

Patience is going to be your best friend while you're starting or growing your business. You're going to want to jump into everything and knock all your goals out the way. The more you progress, the more you'll be tested so it'll be important to take a second to breathe. This is where remembering that there's no such thing as an overnight success will come into play. Work and patience will be equally important before your "big break." God will give you your blessings when you're ready for them, so all you have to do is have faith and prepare.

Give your brand and yourself some time to sow the ground, which will ensure a strong harvest. Taking the time to prepare your business to meet any challenge isn't simply a good idea, it will also guarantee that you're ready to level up. For example, I bought a larger warehouse than I needed at the time because I had faith that my business would grow to fill the space. KHP grew beyond what most people expected, but I was prepared and I had the space it needed to flourish.

Being patient also means embracing the learning experiences that come with each part of the journey, so enjoy the lessons. You'll be managing your business as well as your private life, family and relationships. Because that comes with stress, you'll be in situations where you'll be inclined to react to people instead of listening. When you react, you tend to make decisions that you may regret. Practicing patience will help you pick up the habit of processing something rather than immediately responding, which always yields better results.

I exercise patience through prayer. I pray everyday and start each day by giving thanks to God. If I know I'm going to have a difficult conversation with someone, I first ask to pray with them, and I pray to God to help the person understand where I'm coming from and what my hope is for him or her.

## TAKE THE TIME TO BUILD YOUR PRODUCT

I've already discussed that your business's success will depend on having a product people want and understanding the product's place in the market. The common factor between these two things? Research!

Creating a product people want to buy is one of the most basic business concepts, but surprisingly, very few people understand this. I'm always confused when people launch a product without testing it or trying to figure out if consumers want it. Why waste time and money on something people might not be interested in buying? Many potential business owners get so caught up thinking they have the next best thing that they don't take the time to understand the market. They can tell you what they think, but they don't know their numbers. Even when they share stories of people asking for their product, they use family members as examples, which means they haven't really "sold" the idea outside of their immediate family.

Your family may be a convenient place to start thinking about who would buy your product, but it can't be the entirety of your market research. If you believe you have an idea worth pursuing, you can't be afraid to look at the competition and understand what it's offering so you know how to stand out. Also, you have to get feedback on your product to find out how you can compete in the market.

To figure out if your product is viable, see if you can answer the questions below. If you can't, you may need to do more research or reevaluate some part of your product idea.

**Pro Tip:** You can use these answers to develop your marketing and sales pitch.

- What problem are you trying to solve with your product?
- Who does your product help?
- Is there a cheaper or free option already on the market?
- Are you priced too high or too low and, in determining the price, did you consider all your costs?

- How is your product better than what's currently on the market?
- Who are your local competitors and how big is your market?

Truth be told, your product could be great. But there may only be three people in your local community who want to buy it. Social media would allow you to grow your target market. However, you then have to consider the work involved in marketing your product on that scale and understand the investment and the logistics required to ship it.

Here are some things to keep in mind when you're considering the shipping of your product:

How are you going to support international requests?
- Not all postal providers ship to all places.
- The cost of shipping to certain parts of the world may make your product cost undesirable. Do you want to close off shipping to that part of the world or seek other options such as partnering with a local provider?

How will you determine if there is enough need to ship nationally or internationally?

Does your product have a customs cost associated with it?

Can you ship your product by air?
- Products containing certain chemicals that are on the US Hazardous Materials list usually have to be shipped by land.

Does your product need additional packaging?
- For example, is it fragile?

How long will it take to ship your product and how will customers track orders?

How much inventory are you willing to hold?
- This is especially important to know as there's a fine balance between selling out and having too much inventory that can expire.

Figuring out these logistical details is an integral part of growing your business.

I'll be honest, social media spoiled me a bit. In the beginning, I was going with the flow and because of social media, I moved fast. I started with my product Sleek Edge. I already knew there was a demand for it because I worked in the salon and saw my clients struggle with finding pomade that held down their edges. The market was there and sales were happening in the shop. I was able to use that knowledge to test out Sleek Edge on some of my clients and on myself. I then took the feedback and worked with it until the product had the right formulation.

As Kaleidoscope continues to expand, I've become more cautious and aware of the need to analyze each product and each move. I now watch a product to understand people's buying behavior. Is there a demand for it all year or a particular time of the year when it sells more? When should I hold more inventory of the product? How can I make the directions reader-friendly so people find the product easy to use?

Just like creating and launching a business is all about answering a whole lot of questions, same goes for a product. If you're going to enter this world, be ready to do research, research and more research. What I'm not telling you to do, however, is wait until you create the perfect product. There is no such thing. You produce a good product and then you keep improving it. Waiting for perfection is exhausting and usually results in never launching the product. Perfection is just an excuse. Don't be afraid to try.

## CREATING A SALES AND GROWTH STRATEGY

It's easy to think that your current situation dictates your future. Trust me, the Lord has not left you anywhere without a path out. All you have to do is be courageous enough to take the first step.

Developing a sales and growth strategy is one of those steps you have to take, and it'll help you increase your sales and your business. A sales and growth strategy is a good way to plan for the future while taking stock of where you are right now. In some ways, it is similar to the SMART-R goals you developed in Chapter 4. It provides clear goals that can be measured and evaluated.

**A sales and growth strategy:**
- clearly outlines the future vision of the business;
- develops key priorities and outcomes;
- provides guidelines for engaging with potential clients; and
- determines short and long-term goals for the business.

Once you create your strategy, isn't set in stone. As you learn more about your business, your customers and the industry, you'll constantly be evaluating and updating it.

In essence, developing your strategy can be broken down into three key steps.

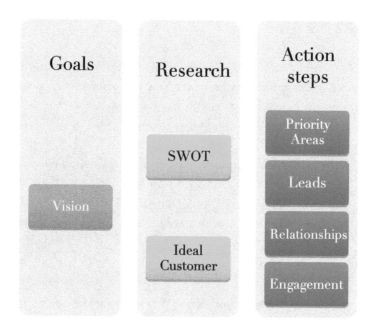

## STEP 1: DETERMINE YOUR GOALS

When you build a strategy, you're creating an action plan that will move you towards your goal. So, first and foremost, you should know what that is.

- **Creating a vision:** Where do you want your business to go? What does your business look like five years from now? Not sure? Look back at the vision board exercises you did in Chapters 1 and 3. Your goal should be the biggest, craziest idea you can think of for your business's future 'cause I guarantee, you ain't thinking as big as the Lord (not yet at least).

## STEP 2: RESEARCH

Remember how I said that if you don't like researching, you won't like being an entrepreneur? Now that your vision is clear, you have to figure out what you have and what you're missing. So, take the time to do some more research.

- **Your ideal customer:** I've talked about understanding your target market. Now, I want you to take that one step further and think about what your ideal customer looks like. What does he or she do? Why would this person want your product? How old is he or she? I want you to build a profile of the person.

- **Do a SWOT analysis:** SWOT stands for Strengths, Weaknesses, Opportunities and Threats. It's a high-level way of looking at your business to see what makes it unique and likely to succeed and also what can put it at risk of failure. A SWOT analysis will also help you identify people in your life who can help you get your product out. You can download free SWOT templates online that include other questions to consider.

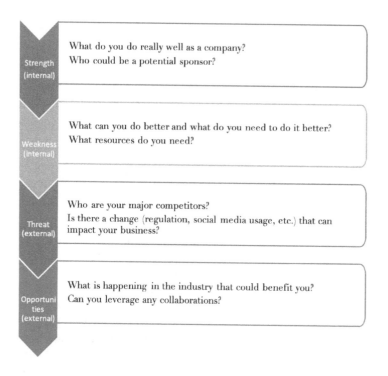

Strength (internal)
What do you do really well as a company?
Who could be a potential sponsor?

Weakness (internal)
What can you do better and what do you need to do it better?
What resources do you need?

Threat (external)
Who are your major competitors?
Is there a change (regulation, social media usage, etc.) that can impact your business?

Opportunities (external)
What is happening in the industry that could benefit you?
Can you leverage any collaborations?

## STEP 3: START TAKING ACTION

The thing about having all this information is you have to act on it. A SWOT analysis and developing your ideal customer profile should lead you to identifying prospects to build and grow your business.

- **Priority areas:** What areas of your business do you need to focus on before you get your first client? Do you have the resources in place (time, money, people) to support your clients? Do you have your product priced? Have you figured out all shipping and payment details?

- **Leads:** Look at your circle of friends, family, acquaintances, mentors and the people or organizations who are 1) potential clients and 2) can introduce you to potential clients. Take stock of the people you interact with and the people in your life. Also, examine the events you attend or should be attending to connect with potential clients.

- **Relationships:** A large part of your growth strategy is going to be managing relationships. This includes relationships with clients to ensure they're happy and with other industry leaders to build partnerships. You always want to be authentic in your approach to relationships.

- **Engagement:** To market to your ideal clients, you need to know how they engage with the world and how you'll engage with them. Are they all on social media? If they have a concern, how will they get in touch with you? Is email communication the preferred form of contact? Understanding how your ideal customers behave will help you craft the right message and employ the most effective delivery method.

## OPPORTUNITY IS EVERYWHERE!

Once you understand your product's place in the market, it's time to start thinking about how you're going to get it into the "right hands." That means clients, investors and sponsors—essentially the people who are going to use your product, invest in your product or recommend your product. Opportunities exist everywhere, but you have to be ready to act at any moment and unearth them. Your SWOT analysis and ideal customer profile should help you determine some places you can connect with your target market, but also be open to unexpected opportunities.

A short while ago, I was on a panel with a few other speakers at Dillard University. It wasn't a paid conference or a significantly large event, but I decided I wanted to speak to these students and share my story. Truth be told, I don't think even 10 percent of them knew who I was. I was just a lady who had created a successful business. What I didn't realize was the audience included more than just students. Their mentors were there as well. After the panel speeches, one of the mentors spoke with me and we connected when he told me how much he enjoyed the stuff I was doing and that he liked how I inspired the audience. I was glad that people had gotten something from it.

A few days later, he called me up and said, "I think you'd be great for an event Essence is organizing. I told them about you and they'd love to talk to you." When I got on the phone with Essence, they told me, "He spoke so highly about you and we were so intrigued that we did some research. We're impressed." The opportunity to speak at an Essence event is not something I would have ever imagined. It came out of a decision to share my story with a few hundred students.

What I'm trying to get you to see is that you must treat every chance as an opportunity for brand and business growth. You have to be ready to take an opportunity and make it yours. I could have turned down the Dillard University speaking engagement but, instead I decided to share with these students that God has a vision for them and they need to have faith and follow it. While I went there without expectations, the Lord had other ideas and blessed me so that I stood out. The impression I created led me to appear at the Essence event in Nola.

I thought that would be the end of it, but then The Today Show found me because of Essence's write-up about the event. Sharing my story on national television? Wow, that was another level of blessing I didn't expect. If you take an action, no matter how small, with good intention, it always comes back to you in ways you never expected.

By not hiding from God's blessings, I've been able to make great connections at this point. The people who have recently come into my life have been key figures in changing my life's direction. While I've always relied on myself, I now have an abundance of people just teaching me things.

## NETWORKING YOUR NET WORTH

I want to show you that getting out there and connecting with people isn't as scary as it seems. When you're authentic, you attract people who are genuinely interested in supporting you and your business. Building a strong network isn't just important to your sales and growth strategy, it's also a resource to find mentors, peers and a potential support system. For example, I have a lot of great friends who aren't as involved in the social media world. While they give an ear when I need it, they can't really offer advice about an influencer issue or a social media concern. That's one of the times when my network is important. It's about having people you can reach out to who are in the industry and understand your struggles.

I've met some of my best friends from networking and collabs. These are relationships that began as mutually beneficial partnerships but evolved as I got to know the people on a personal level. Networking, in the simplest terms, is just like making friends when you were a kid. Don't network with people you don't want to hang out with. You'll end up miserable and hating anything associated with them. You don't have to be best friends with everyone in your network but you gotta like them. When you like them, you're more inclined to want to work with them, inspire each other to come up with great ideas and have fun while building your brand.

Get out and start connecting with people whenever you can. If you're shy, start with a smaller event or a place where you feel comfortable, such as your church. Eventually, surround yourself with other entrepreneurs. One way to do that is through the Meetup app. The app allows you to search by topic and city to meet up with others who are interested in the same topic. You can organize a meet-up or attend one hosted by someone else. There are meet-ups of all kinds for hobbyists, small business owners, women, Black women, millennials and more. They're a great way to start, if you feel like networking at a larger more formal event will overwhelm you.

If you feel like you can handle more significant events, check out those created by the Business Improvement Associations (BIAs) in your area or by your university or college alumni associations. These organizations usually have a more extensive network and will allow you to connect with more people. Additionally, there are many professional associations you can join that, on top of organizing networking events, usually have subsidized professional development programs for their members. For example, there are more than 10 national African-American professional associations in the U.S.

If face-to-face networking isn't your thing, that's okay. With social media, you have so many ways to connect. Slide into people's DMs, comment on a post or suggest they check out your page. You can pre-write a bunch of introductions to help you break the ice.

The thing is, if you're shy, no matter how good your product is, only a limited amount of people will hear about it. Hold your head up high and don't be afraid to offer your merchandise to people. You're helping them find a solution to an issue they have. They may have been looking for something like your product! Don't pass up that opportunity.

## NETWORKING EVENT ESSENTIALS

Have your elevator pitch ready: This is a 30-second pitch about who you are and your product. It should also include details on the problem your product solves.

- **Look the part:** When you're meeting potential investors, you want to appear as someone they would want to trust their money to. Be conscious of how you look. That means you need to consider everything from posture and body language to clothes and makeup. Some events are more formal than others. Make sure you're aware of the dress code, so you don't stand out for the wrong reasons.

- **Relax and smile:** People are drawn to those who seem positive and friendly because they appear more confident. If you aren't confident yet, I'll say it again: Faith it till you make it. Find a way to calm your mind, whether that means taking a few deep breaths or dragging your friend along so you have support. Find a technique to ground yourself and get ready to face the situation.

- **Know where to send them:** If people want to learn more, direct them to an up-to-date website or social media page with current contact information. Make sure you don't send anyone to that email you forget to check or a blog that hasn't been updated in three months. Ensure all your content is relevant and you're responding to people within 48 hours.

- **Do your research:** If you're going to an event that has made the speakers or attendees list public, identify the people you want to speak to. It'll save you time and energy. Additionally, it'll make you look professional when you personalize your pitch to their product needs.

- **Build relationships and follow up:** Swap business cards and contact information, and set up a coffee date or an informational interview. Even if certain people you meet at the event don't require your product now, you never know what can change and who is in their network. Beyond the event, establish and maintain a relationship with them, and offer help and advice where you can. People always remember how others offered to help them.

## BE OPTIMISTIC IN OPPOSITION

Running a small business is all about being a leader, and that means not only sharing your vision but also maintaining a positive outlook. Your first few social media posts or videos may not gain much traction, but as the brand's leader you have to keep creating. Your team and supporters are looking at you to lead the way. Always show your followers, supporters and investors that you have faith in your vision.

Once you have a team, you must lead by example and always bring your a-game—no matter what's happening around you. When I moved my fulfillment out of New Orleans, I ended up facing a lot of issues with my warehouse manager. I didn't know it at the time but a few orders had not been shipped. Unshipped orders mean dissatisfied customers and a potential loss of future sales because of the customer not returning, which causes a ding on the company's reputation.

I was scheduled to speak at a Unity in Community event my friend organized in response to the mayor of Kenner, Louisiana banning Nike gear from the city's recreational spaces. It was a massive event with many people supporting my friend, and I was speaking as a New Orleans business owner and resident. It was vital for me to be there for my friend and because I believed in the rally's message. I was at the event with my entire marketing team when I found out about the unfulfilled orders.

I called my warehouse manager and my team could hear me getting into a heated discussion. Hanging up the phone, I was confused, frustrated and upset. We had orders coming in and I didn't want our clients to feel like we were not respecting them and the money they were spending on KHP. Soon, it was time for me to speak. I got up there and made sure that what was going on behind-the-scenes didn't at all show in my face. Later in the day, I got an email from the marketing team letting me how happy and impressed they were that I was able to keep a level head and speak at the event.

The members of my marketing team saw a leader who, despite whatever crisis she faces, will always remain professional and represent the business in the best way possible. It allowed them to have faith in the company and in their decision to work for me. I had no choice. Wearing both business and community leader hats means understanding that no matter how important managing a business situation is, I have to be fully present if I have dedicated myself to a community task. Some of the hardest choices have to be made on the spot, but strong leadership is the cornerstone of maintaining the faith your staff has in you. The person your staff members see is the person they're going to mimic. So, if you ever think you're going to break, break in the privacy of your own home or with your closest and most trusted friend, family member or ally. With your team and in public, leadership should be your default function.

I've been a leader in many ways, so I simply tweaked those experiences to fit the small business arena. My leadership is a reflection of how I was raised and how I manage my family. I was the head of my household since I had children. I set the rules, guidelines and boundaries regarding what they could and couldn't do. My children know I don't like fights in the house, so we've always figured out ways to deal with any situation. I also don't let my children get away with being inconsiderate. For example, they all know that if someone is ordering food delivery, they're responsible for finding out if their siblings (or anyone in the house) wants anything. If they don't, I'll throw out the food, regardless of who ordered it.

In the business world, my rules are the same. I'm big on creating a work environment that's conflict-free, considerate and kind. When we have issues, I mediate or put my staff through conflict resolution. My team knows the workplace is a respectful one and they must be considerate of each other.

Being a leader doesn't mean you have to sign up for leadership courses or get a certificate in it. Though, if you want to do that you should because there are some excellent courses on managing people. You're a leader in many aspects of your life already and you may not even recognize it. You're a leader as a parent, when you're managing your family or organizing events, or even in the workplace. You just need to embrace those skills and apply them to your small business. Leadership is about understanding yourself as a person and creating an environment in which you and your staff can thrive.

# Chapter 8

## BUILDING IN A DIGITAL AGE

Let me give you the most important piece of advice upfront: Don't be boring!

I don't understand why everyone is obsessed with fitting in and being the same when the Lord made you to stand out. He didn't make a mistake when He made you. Instead, He created someone unique and special. It's this uniqueness He wants you to share with the world. Get excited about being who you are.

I attribute a large part of my brand's growth to the fact that it's just me having fun, being creative with the imagination God granted me and giving people a reason to laugh. My followers, my Instagram community, are with me because they see someone they can relate to. They know my story, my intentions, what I've done and my commitment to giving back. We're so afraid that people will laugh at us if we don't look like we have the perfect life that we're scared to do anything different. But that's where the authentic connections happen. So, live a little, laugh a little and have fun with your social media.

While creating, always examine what you could be doing to change and improve your content. Experiment with some new styles, make a video instead of a taking photo, take a chance and make a post based on that crazy idea you had, post a popular meme but make it your own. There's nothing wrong with reposting content as long as you credit it, and it reflects the brand you're creating. Don't ask anyone what they think, just do it. Just remember, your content should be clean and friendly.

Also, as I've mentioned before, the most boring thing you can do is copy someone else's idea. When you copy, your outcome will always look second best and not as fresh as it should. Your clients and followers are going to follow you because they like your voice, not Jesseca Dupart's words said in your voice. Building authentic engagement is centered on showing your genuine self. As your audience grows, you'll notice the people who your words resonate with will find your voice.

## THE BASICS

Setting up your social media account is similar to setting up your business in that you need to think about what you want to represent and how you want to represent it. So, you have to put the same thought and effort into your social media account as you do into your business.

- **Be committed:** Understand your vision and what you represent before creating a name, then be ready to invest the time to make it grow. Be specific in what you want to do but don't limit the audience. That means always keeping the bigger picture in mind. Every year, the number of social media users is growing so your account is a gateway to millions of people. If you treat social media like a hobby, so will your followers. I'm not exaggerating when I say, social media should be as important as eating. It's necessary for your survival in the digital age.

- **Be professional:** Make the time to create professional content. At the beginning, you'll have necessary costs you can't avoid. Do the best with what you have. iPhones and Androids take amazing photos. You can look up YouTube videos that will teach you how to make the most out of those devices. As you continue to grow, you can look into upgrading to more professional equipment or hiring professionals for services such as web design and photo shoots.

- **Build your profile:** When you set up your business name, you should also check that it's available on your preferred social media platform(s). Your profile is what people use to determine (in about 10 seconds) if they're going to follow you. During that time, they're looking at four things:

1. **Profile name:** It should be indicative to where you want to be rather than where you currently are. Had I known where I'd be today, I wouldn't have named my Instagram @darealbbjudy. More than likely, it would've been something associated with hair.

2. **Profile picture:** Your display picture should represent the product you're trying to sell. For example, if you're a

hairstylist, you could post a picture of yourself or of the best hairstyle you've ever created.

3.  **Your bio:** Once they make it past the name and photo, most people will check out your profile bio to find out who you are. Keep your bio simple and real. Also, if the social media platform allows you to add a hashtag, insert any that are associated with you or the brand.

My Instagram bio is: #darealbbjudy #miracledrops
CEO @kaleidoscopehairproducts
#kaleidoscopehairproducts
I owe God everything #praythroughtheprocess

Kaleidoscope Hair Products' (KHP) Instagram bio says:
Home of "The Miracle Drop System" We are dedicated to changing lives one head at a time!
#kaleidoscopehairproducts

Both bios are simple and state who we are and what we're committed to. Mine is who I am and reflects my faith in God, while KHP's leverages our most popular item and company vision.

4.  **Your feed:** This is the reason quality matters. People are investing their time and energy into your brand, so they want to see both time and effort reflected in what you post. Sharing different aspects of yourself, your product, the day-to-day workings of your business and motivational quotes can all help different people engage and build your followers. Typically, you get two swipes on social media and then you're out. Think about it, no one goes to the second page of a Google search. Strive to

always have trendy, relevant and exciting content so people aren't so quick to want to leave your profile.

## GO WHERE THE PEOPLE ARE

Understanding where your audience is at and what it connects to is important to maintaining your business. Now, don't get me wrong, finding the right home for my brand's style wasn't easy. I didn't just start on social media and only try Instagram. I actually tried different print and media ads. In fact, one of the biggest funded marketing campaigns I ran early on was an infomercial. When I first launched KHP, I wanted to expand my reach and thought an infomercial would be the way to go. I flew down to Miami and hired a team and actors. The entire thing ended up not working out and flopped, big time. I did that infomercial at a time when I wasn't aware of all the rules, regulations and subtle but important details of creating content for TV. The infomercial wasn't right for me at that time but that doesn't mean it will never be right. I now know a lot more about creating content and understanding how to tell a story. That's the thing about marketing: You can always go back and explore ideas and streams that you may have tried before.

In building KHP, I've done YouTube and Google ads as well as editorials about the products to increase brand awareness. I've experimented and keep experimenting with different marketing streams. However, I know my social media drives business to my site, so KHP's and my social media accounts are always at the forefront of any marketing campaign I develop. Your marketing should never be stagnant. Marketing, especially digital marketing, is always evolving, so stay ahead of the competition by understanding how to make it work for you.

## PRIMP AND PREPARE

You can't plan for everything but you can prepare your business and brand to survive. So, what does preparation look like? Planning and researching, of course. But you knew that already, right?

When everyone was forced to abandon Nola because of Hurricane Katrina, I went to Houston. Before launching my hair business there, I took the time to understand where my clients were and what kind of styles they liked. With an understanding of the market, I was able to look at my portfolio and choose the images that I knew would perform well with my target market. I took those images and created a photo book to show Houston clients my range of work.

Anyone who knows me will tell you two things about me: I am cautious and I am prepared. Even as KHP was pulling in six figures a month, I was still driving my old Tahoe with the side mirror falling off, and my leggings had holes in them. Neither of these things bothered me because, at that moment, my brand was my focus. I wanted to ensure my brand would be able to take care of itself and if that meant sacrificing then I would do without. Sacrificing in the short term will make you big gains in the long term. Driving my old beat up truck around allowed me to save the money I would need to build a buffer for my business. I didn't even look at getting a new car until I had saved a substantial amount of money to buy what my heart desired. That same cautious approach also translated before I decided to launch KHP in retail stores. I did a lot of prep work. Taking a business from online to brick and mortar stores meant thinking about stuff I never had to consider before. I had spreadsheets measuring and analyzing everything. I made sure I had more than enough bottles of Miracle Drops to fill all of our requests plus extra just in case there were any issues. The survival of your business requires you to sacrifice where you need to, dot every I and cross every T, and be ready for the unexpected.

## INTERNET MARKETING BASICS

I could give you a whole bunch of facts about Google Ads, search engine optimization (SEO) and retargeting, but I'm only going to speak on what I know. I've tried out Google Ads, but I hired someone to run that for me. I also hired someone for retargeting and SEO, but I soon realized the highest return on my investment (ROI) came from social media marketing. This is the preferred method that works for KHP. I'm not saying, however, that these tools won't be helpful to your business. So, if these are tactics you'd like to try out, my advice is to seek help from a professional.

Below, in addition to some of the most common marketing tactics, you'll also find some important marketing terms to remember.

- **Ad placement:** Ads are generally placed on the top or down the side of a website. Depending on the location and style of ad (photo or video), cost will vary.

- **Cost per impression (CPI):** The price to run the ad is based on the number of impressions it receives, which is the number of times people view the ad. There are ways to track impressions to ensure you're getting a good ROI.

- **Fixed cost:** Like the name implies, you pay a fixed

amount for your ad to appear for a predetermined length of time. This method is very similar to buying a standard ad in a newspaper or magazine. I would recommend fixed cost for sites you know get a lot of traffic and are well known.

- **Retargeting:** Retargeting is a way to bring interested customers back to your site. In general, the stat is that only two percent of page visits are converted into sales. Retargeting is a way to convert the remaining 98 percent. If someone visits your site and doesn't buy something, a bit of code follows him or her while he or she surfs the web, and your ads start popping up on the various sites the person visits. It keeps your company at the forefront of someone's mind. As with all marketing techniques, when it comes to retargeting measure the number of sales it generates against the cost of setting it up.

- **Landing page:** A landing page is where someone is taken once he or she clicks on an ad. A lot of businesses default this to the company homepage. Bad idea. If someone clicks on an ad for Miracle Drops, he or she expects to land right on a page about Miracle Drops rather than having to search an entire website for the product. Our ads take customers right to our product page, where they can quickly add a couple bottles of Miracle Drops to their cart, check out and be on their way.

- **Return on investment (ROI):** Every marketing campaign should yield a good ROI. That's why it's essential to track the number of sales, clicks to your website and interest each ad generates. Tracking your ROI is a good way to see what ads and ad placements work for you.

- **Search engine optimization (SEO):** SEO helps to ensure that search engines such as Google are able to quickly find your site. The sooner a search engine finds your site, the higher up it will be on the results page. Most people generally look at the top five results, so it's essential that your site is one of them. SEO is a combination of using the right keywords and phrases in your site content and building the website in a way that allows search engines to find it easily and quickly. If you outsource your website development, hire someone who is knowledgeable about SEO.

When it comes to placing ads, tracking to see how they are doing is key. I analyze all of my campaigns from the get-go. With The Edge Police, for example, we incorporated commercials into the series. The response (in sales of KHP) was so huge that with just the first episode, the series had paid for itself.

Your ROI, however, isn't always going to be about money. With bigger productions such as Judy Wonka and Judy Springer, we had a much bigger production budget so I knew the ROI wasn't going to be as high. I still wanted to do them because they were fun and a new creative way to work with creators and get the brand out there. For both series, I factored in the value from the increased visibility for KHP as being a positive ROI and reason enough to do them. That said, I know sometimes I can get carried away with an idea and the need to have it turn out exactly as I want it. To balance myself, I've surrounded myself with people who are paying attention to that stuff.

Your marketing budget can easily get out of control, especially with digital marketing. Impressions are important but those impressions must convert into sales. Otherwise, it's just money down the drain. Here is a calculation to help you figure it out.

Calculating cost per impression: (usually calculated per 1000 visitors)

**Cost of the ad ÷ Total # of impressions × 1000=     CPI**

If it cost you $16 per 1,000 visitors but 1,000 visitors aren't getting your more than $16, you'll have to rethink both the marketing strategy and your landing page.

| Marketing campaign | Cost | Total impressions | CPI (per 1,000) | Total sales | Campaign value (yes/no) | Comments (issues with campaign; timing) |
|---|---|---|---|---|---|---|
| *E.g. Facebook post* | $24 | *4,300 (approx.)* | *$5.5 (24/4300 x 1000)* | *$400* | *No* | *- Spent $5.5 to make $4.* *- Sales didn't convert* *- Issue with partner* |

Running an analysis on your marketing campaigns and plan will help you realign your strategy and website based on client needs. Below is an example of how to analyze a marketing campaign.

Even though on the surface this campaign made money, the ROI isn't that great. The sale or event only yielded $400. And while it's more money than you invested, the dollar return per impression isn't very high (about 40 cents per impression). Sometimes, you may feel like because you made some money, the ad was worth it. However, when you think about marketing, you also have to consider if the ad could have done better. Was this the best return you could have gotten for your investment?

Here are some reasons a marketing campaign may not work:

- **You chose the wrong approach:** An example of this is selling a weight loss pill by fat shaming people on social media rather than showing before and after photos or having customers share their journey.

- **You chose the wrong placement:** An example of this is when I paid a lot of money for a celebrity who is bald by choice to promote Miracle Drops and none of the person's followers even cared.

- **You chose the wrong posting time:** An example of this is posting a Thursday lunch special at 5 pm on Wednesday! Pay attention to your customer insights and what the hell you're promoting. I know common sense isn't so common, but I've seen a lot of this over the years.

- **Great campaign, poor planning:** You can't create a campaign around the release of a new product if you haven't even received the items in stock yet. It's almost as if you're setting yourself up for failure.

Understanding the reasons why your campaign didn't work will help you to convert future campaigns into sales.

## MARKET TO THE MASSES

Developing a marketing plan will help you reach the most people with (hopefully) the least amount of money, maximizing your ROI.

The process of creating a marketing plan will pull in the information we looked at when you defined your target market. A marketing plan actually requires more in-depth thinking about your target audience. Understanding your ideal customer and target market will help you identify places and opportunities to connect with your audience. For example, try to figure out information such as average income and education level—not because you want "wealthy" or "smart" clients, but because that kind of information will help you figure out the sites that they're more likely to frequent.

As I mentioned before, I saw myself as part of my target market, so I asked myself some real questions about how I shop, what makes me interested in a product and what would make me buy it. The answers to these questions helped me figure out how I wanted to talk about the benefits of our products.

Some of the questions in the template below may not feel relevant to your business or brand and others may have more than one answer. The template should, however, help you think about developing a plan. It's not the only way and it isn't absolute truth. Adjust it and play with it until it helps you.

Also, keep in mind that as you build your followers, your advertising costs may go down because you'll have a direct line to your target market. Your production costs, on the other hand, will go up. People always want bigger and better things, so as your followers grow so does the expected quality of work.

Here are some tips I encourage you to think about when creating your marketing plan.

## MARKETING PLAN TEMPLATE

**Part A: Marketing Plan Goal**

1. **The goal of my marketing plan is to:**

- Generate more sales
- Gain new customers
- Reconnect with existing customers
- Get existing customers to buy a new product
- Launch a new product
- Build brand loyalty
- Increase brand awareness
- Customer appreciation
- Increase engagement
- Build market share

No matter what the goal of your marketing plan is, you should always keep an eye on increasing your sales. All of the goals I've outlined above are focused on growing your business. Some of the goals are more straightforward in terms of increasing sales and others are focused on creating behaviors in your clients to increase your sales.

When making a marketing plan goal, I look at year-to-date sales. From there, I go back and remember what I did to achieve those sales and how I could have increased them. I'd be lying if I told you that I set clear goals of, for example, wanting to increase sales by 20 percent. I don't operate from a step-by-step rulebook.

2.   **Determine a budget.** It can be a percentage or an actual cost. For example, you could dedicate 10 percent of every month's sales to marketing. The general average, by the way, is about five to 10 percent. Please note though, determining a budget can be a little tricky. When starting KHP and bringing The Edge Police to life, for example, we got our costumes from Party City and Goodwill. We didn't use any special cameras or equipment either; most of the series was shot on a smart phone. I say that to say, don't break the bank if you don't have to. My biggest budgeting suggestion is that you spend the money you feel comfortable parting with. As you grow, you may find yourself in situations that require you to overextend the budget. Only do this if you're sure you'll have a bigger ROI.

My annual budget for marketing and promotions is:

_____

**Part B: Client Profile**

3.  **Profile of my ideal customer**
i.  Age:

- 2-17
- 18-24
- 25-34
- 35-44
- 45-54
- 55-64
- 65+

ii.  Gender:

- Male
- Female
- Both

iii.  Income level:

- Under $19,999
- $20,000 - $39,999
- $40,000 - $69,999
- $70,000 - $99,999
- $100,000+

iv.   Education level:

- Some high school
- High school graduate
- Some university/college
- University or college degree
- Master's
- Ph.D.

## 4.   What would interest my ideal client?

Think about hobbies, news and fashion as well as what your ideal client does for fun and for work. Come up with five interests.

E.g. Entrepreneur:

v.    _____

vi.   _____

vii.  _____

viii. _____

ix.   _____

## 5.   My ideal client is most likely to use the following social media sites:

- Twitter
- Facebook
- WeChat
- QQ
- Google+

- Instagram
- Pinterest
- LinkedIn
- YouTube
- Tumblr
- Reddit
- Snapchat
- Quora
- Mediu

**6. My ideal client is most likely to visit these websites:**

You can answer this based on the how you responded to the above questions or other things you've determined about your ideal client.

| Client Profile | Potential Site |
|---|---|
| **E.g. Entrepreneur** | *Forbes* |
| **E.g. On trend** | *Buzzfeed* |

**Part C: Making a Plan**

7.   Look at the websites on your list as potential places to advertise by considering if it's worth your time and money to do so. That list you just created in number six is gonna lead you to a lot of potential opportunities but you won't have the time, money and energy to advertise with all of them (nor should you, really).

Using the questions below as a starting point, rank the

websites you've identified to see where it makes sense to spend your money, what is most affordable and within your price range, and what will result in the most reach. This step will require you to reach out to the websites' public relations and/or marketing team to get estimates.

- How much does it cost?
- How much work will it be to create a post/story?
- How much of a reach will you get for your ideal client?
- Is there a cheaper or less time-consuming option?
- Is it meeting the goals of your marketing plan?
- Do you have a contact at the company?

| Site | Ad Opport- unity | Potential Cost | Estimated Impressions | Contact Info | Rank |
|------|------|------|------|------|------|
| **Forbes** | Banners | $500+ | | | |
| **Buzzfeed** | Create a post | Time to write and craft an op-ed | | | |
| **Instagram** | Promote post | $24 | | | |
| **Email campaigns** | Email followers | Time and opportunit y cost | | | |

## TIMING IS EVERYTHING

What's the best time to run your campaign? Let's look at the case of sales. Typically, sales are great to have closer to the weekend, which is payday for many Americans. Make sure you consider large sales on days when people expect to get a deal. In the U.S., that might be Black Friday. (Side note: Always remember to make sure your inventory is locked in tight. It's important to monitor inventory when planning for major sales). If, however, you're not going to run a special during that time, don't advertise. Yes, people may visit your site but if they come expecting a sale and see nothing, they are more likely to be turned off. That doesn't mean you have to do what everyone else is doing either. You can, for example, have a sale on your birthday.

Potential dates for ad or sales:

_____

8.   **Do you need support to run this campaign?**

- What skills do you need?
- Can you hire people with the skills you need? If so, from where?
- What will it cost you?
- Who will be responsible for maintaining contact and making sure the work is completed?

**PART D: Sales Impact**

To really understand the cost of each campaign, you have to see the, hopefully positive, impact on your sales.

**9. To measure that impact:**

- create a sales increase goal to work towards;
- track sales leading to the campaign launch, during the campaign period and post campaign; and

- if possible, compare sales from the same time last year (and previous years if you have those numbers). This will give you an idea of your growth rate over each year.

At the end of the year, use this information to see what campaign resulted in the greatest sales increase. Then, challenge yourself and create stretch goals for your campaigns. If you had a five percent increase in sales with your last campaign, why not try for 15 percent with then next one?

Creating estimated sales goals will also help you develop better campaigns and hold you accountable to your campaign budget. If your campaign didn't result in the sales you had predicted, brainstorm possible reasons for the shortfall. If your campaign did better than expected, look for the reasons that may have assisted in this. A lot of marketing is also dependent on what's happening around us and how people feel. Pay attention to what's making news and how that can impact your sales.

### PART E: Troubleshoot

**10. Plan ahead but always review your marketing plans.** In your marketing plan review, include your estimated sales increases for each campaign and the actual sales. Keeping track of each campaign's performance will help you determine if you need to increase or decrease the number of campaigns you do in a year. My campaigns are usually short series because, as much as I enjoy doing them, I want to move onto the next thing. If you feel like you've done too many sales, stop and try something else or take a break.

That said though, and as much as I talk about being prepared, nothing prepares you for your campaign being better received than you anticipated. When I ran out of inventory for my 2018 Black Friday sale, I had to kick it into high gear to get more product into my warehouses ASAP.

Below is just an idea of how you can track your marketing. I also use my vision board to see what I want to do throughout the year.

| Quarter | Date | Sales/Ad | Cost | Estimated Sales | Goal |
|---------|------|----------|------|-----------------|------|
| Q1 | January | New Year Refresh | N/A -- Instagram | 15 percent over last year | Encourage people to restock after the holidays |
| Q1 | February | Launch book – Instagram and Amazon | | 20 percent of followers | Introduce a new product |

# WHEN THE MIRACLE DROPS

# Chapter 9
## QUEENS SUPPORTING QUEENS

That level playing field social media and the internet have created should be used to your advantage. Today, building a business and a brand is about making real connections with people. I'm your average girl but social media gave me to chance to show people my personality and what Kaleidoscope Hair Products (KHP) has to offer. I didn't have to rely on a middleman or someone else to move my product. It was, and still is, on me! I'm able to continuously experiment and connect to my market.

Throughout my social media journey, I've met, collaborated and mentored so many queens. The opportunities social media created for me have already opened the door to me sharing my knowledge through various avenues, including a speaking tour. I've been able to uplift and support women who are all about changing the game and taking back and creating their own spaces. I love sharing my blessings with my sisters because I know that's what the Lord wants me to do. It's a part of who I am and what Kaleidoscope, as a brand, stands behind.

## LET'S TALK SOCIAL MEDIA

As great as it is, social media can be overwhelming. Many new sites pop up all the time and keeping track of them can be its own job. As you know though, social media is a necessary part of any small business and its marketing strategy.

Below I have demographical information for some of the top social media sites in the U.S.A. Use this info as a starting point to help you consider the best site for you. I've included the number of users, as of 2018.

## POPULAR U.S.A. SOCIAL MEDIA SITES

| Social Media Site | How Do You Engage? | Key Demographics | | Age of Most Users | Number of Users |
|---|---|---|---|---|---|
| | | Gender (% of population that uses the site, USA) | | | |
| Facebook | Posts and stories | Men | 75% | 18-34 | 2.27 billion |
| | | Women | 83% | | |
| Instagram | Photos, short videos, stories | Men | 26% | 18-29 | 1 billion |
| | | Women | 36% | | |
| YouTube | Videos | Men | 83% | 18-49 | 1.3 billion |
| | | Women | 83% | | |
| Snapchat | Short videos and photos | Men | 30% | 18-24 | 300 million |
| | | Women | 70% | | |
| LinkedIn | Posts | Men | 31% | 18-49 | 476 million |
| | | Women | 27% | | |
| Pinterest | Pins to external sources | Men | 17% | 18-34 | 250 million |
| | | Women | 45% | | |
| Twitter | 140-character posts | Men | 21% | 18-29 | 33 million |
| | | Women | 21% | | |

https://www.statista.com/statistics/264810/number-of-monthly-active-facebook-users-worldwide/

https://www.statista.com/statistics/253577/number-of-monthly-active-instagram-users/

https://www.statista.com/statistics/810461/us-youtube-reach-gender/

https://merchdope.com/youtube-stats/

https://merchdope.com/youtube-stats/

https://www.statista.com/statistics/810461/us-youtube-reach-gender/

https://www.omnicoreagency.com/snapchat-statistics/

https://www.statista.com/statistics/274050/quarterly-numbers-of-linkedin-members/

https://www.statista.com/statistics/463353/pinterest-global-mau/

https://blog.hootsuite.com/twitter-statistics/

If you're interested in a platform, investigate it a bit further. There's a lot of information online about each platform's users and their profile, which will help you to determine if the site is right for you. A simple online search will bring up a lot of relevant information, including the best suggested post times, the income levels of users and so on.

Remember though, simply because a site has a large reach doesn't necessarily mean it's the right one for you. For example, creating a high-quality video for YouTube requires video production skills, or the time to acquire them, or the money to hire someone to create your video for you. Also, don't forget to track where you're getting the most engagement from.

Eventually, you'll need to be on the sites most applicable to your business and engage with users on all of them. There are many apps and websites that can assist with cross-posting your ads and information on different social media platforms. You may also eventually be at a point where you're ready to hire a marketing team to help you manage the various sites.

Even if you aren't quite ready to use a particular platform, I'd still recommend opening your company's profile. This will prevent others from taking the name and/or using your name to try to sell their products once your company has clout. You can fully launch the profile when you're ready, and if you change your mind and don't want to use a profile after you've created it, deactivate it or reroute the link to one of your active profile pages.

The sites in the chart above are popular in the U.S. If your audience is more international, you may have to look into what sites are popular in the regions you're interested in. For example,

India has the most Facebook users and the U.S.A. has the second highest number of users. So, adapt your social media strategy based on who you'd like to market to or where you want your business to go.

I typically find that when people think of social media, they don't necessarily see their website or blog as part of that group. Your website is where people will go to buy your product or get to know more about you, so it's essential.

*A few tips to get you started online:*

- Own your site address (URL): Invest the money necessary to buy your company URL. You can start with free websites but they usually contain the hosting company's name and then your company name (e.g. http://wordpress."companyname".com). This type of URL doesn't give your company legitimacy.

- Keep it simple: Forget any random underscores, symbols, numbers and extra letters. People won't be able to find you if they can't figure out how to spell your name. Creating a simple name is actually my top rule for social media profiles and websites.

- Hire a professional: A good website developer will know the required SEO to make your site searchable.

- Use a hosting site: A hosting site will allow you to buy your name and set up your site. When you buy your URL from a hosting site rather than a blog site, there are also usually customer service reps who can help you fix any issues that may arise.

- Use blogging site add-ins and tools: All blogging sites give you the option of add-ins or tools to help you manage your blog. You'll get access to everything from integrating your social media platforms to managing your visitor comments.

    1. Use tags in your blog posts to help people find related content on your website.

## REACH, RELIABILITY AND RECIPROCITY

Social media is a tool. It's not the be all end all of anything you're creating, but it is the most powerful and effective way to get your brand noticed. And while social media can help grow and develop your business, it can't take the place of creating a good product. If you have a good product, social media is simply going to help you let others know about it.

### Content

- **Make your posts your own:** People will follow you for your unique voice and not for how well you copy others. You should always have more authentic content than sponsored posts or posts you're sponsoring. People don't want to see ads; they want to connect with real people and brands.

- **Know your audience:** The content I create for KHP's Instagram page is artistic and edited. For the most part, the posts are finished photos, ads or quotes with a simple font and the company logo on a white background. The posts for @darealbbjudy, meanwhile, have a more casual feel. Quotes on that account, for example, can be screen shots from my iPhone Notes app with thoughts I wanted to share. The photos aren't always finished because they're often taken behind-the-scenes. These Instagram accounts' distinct styles are based on the type of engagement followers expect and what they expect from a personal versus company and/or brand account. As you create content, make sure it resonates with your followers and reflects the brand.

- Create a consistent look: Use the same logo and color palette across your digital footprint. iluvcolors.com is very clean with a white background and a rainbow ombré. That look is replicated on KHP's Instagram, and my personal Instagram is inverse but very similar. Photos can be similar but I prefer to not use the exact same photo. Photos and captions should complement each other to build and showcase a consistent brand message across all your sites.

## POSTING

- There are two very distinct social media post types.

2. **Product:** These posts are related to the item you're selling and highlight your product's benefits and unique features. They can include ads, and reviews by other influencers, your clients and users.

3. **Personality:** These are posts that help your followers connect to you as an individual. They may be tips you want to share, moments from your everyday life or questions you pose to your followers to create an interactive experience. These posts are less about selling a product and more about building a genuine connection with your online community.

## HASHTAGS

- I love hashtags! They're a great way to promote your business and tie a theme in with your brand.

- I use two types of hashtags:

1. **Personal hashtags**

o    This is a hashtag you create, and it's important to make sure no one else is using it. It's the hashtag followers, collaborators and peers can click to see your body of work. It's how you differentiate your work posts from life or motivational posts. This hashtag is dedicated to product and not necessarily your personality. KHP's personal hashtags are #MiracleDrops #KaleidoscopeHairProducts.

o   A similar example is the hashtag #KHPVideo, which brings up videos of people we've worked with. When I pursued a video collaboration with Serena Williams, she wanted to know who else had done a video with us. Because we created this hashtag, I was able to show her. It saved me from having to scroll through my page and all my posts to look for past collaborations.

o   #PrayThroughTheProcess, meanwhile, is a hashtag I use for my personality posts. Through it, I share what I've learned from the Lord and my own lessons. I know people who click on that hashtag may be in a dark place and need advice and faith. This isn't an opportunity to sell them hair products. It's a chance to remind them they can overcome anything.

2.   **Hashtags for reach**

o   Popular hashtags are great for extending the reach of your product and getting exposure. These hashtags are usually linked to a location or a theme such as #NewOrleans or #MondayMotivation.

o   Hashtags for reach should also reflect the areas you live and work. So, if you're a hair stylist and you live in New York, applicable hashtags would include: #NYCHairStylist, #NewYorkHairStylist, #NewJerseyHairStylist, #NJHairStylist. If you travel to another city to work, make sure you're using a hashtag related to that location as well.

o   These hashtags are important because they help you get more visibility, resulting in potential customers. The people who click these hashtags are interested in a topic or skill and want to see what people are doing. They may not yet be loyal to a brand or an influencer.

- ■    Instagram has an option to follow hashtags. If someone follows a hashtag, Instagram will put high engagement posts in his or her feed, whether he or she is following that account. This is a great opportunity for your business to get some visibility without you buying an ad.

- ●    Pay attention to spelling. I don't just mean typos, though you don't want to make spelling mistakes either. I mean the way the hashtag is spelled. #NYHairStylist has something like 124,000 posts on Instagram, which is an excellent reach. #NYHairStylists (with an s) only has 2,000 posts. Most people are going to click on the hashtag with more posts.

- ●    Mix and match hashtags because there is no one right formula. Try different combinations of hashtags or new ones to see what increases audience engagement. The ones that work may not be the more popular ones, so sometimes it might be worth using #NYHairStylists instead. See what commonly used hashtags exist for your sector.

- ●    Hashtags should relate to the post. For example, you can't use the hashtag #NolaHairStylist under a post about your kid's first birthday.

## POSTING TIME

- The time you post on social media is important, but timing can be tricky depending on the type of content you're posting. I would never tell you to Google this information because it takes trial and error. My suggestion is to start out by posting at breakfast, lunch and dinner for seven straight days. During this period, watch the engagement of your followers and decide which time is most beneficial for you. Sometimes, videos get better engagement in the evening compared to the morning. Whereas, if you're posting a flyer for a sale, you may receive better engagement in the morning.

o    If you're wondering, as a general rule, social media posts tend to do better in the day, between 5 and 8 pm on weekdays. There is usually very little engagement on Sundays. These popular times, however, will vary by social media platform and by your content, so do some research.

## TRACKING ENGAGEMENT

- Check your posts to see when you get the most engagement. For example, you may decide to post an inspirational video for entrepreneurs on Monday morning and notice you got a higher engagement on it. You can then take that information to create another inspirational video on a different subject and continue to post like content on Monday mornings.

Most social media platforms show you the analytics for your page, which will tell you:

o    your most engaging posts on any given day;

o    the demographics of your followers; and

o    when you get the most engagement.

o    Some sites, such as Instagram, will only offer this option for business profiles.

- The engagement and insights you get on social media sites are always changing. As your audience grows, so will the way they behave. Your followers may go from being majority women to including men. In addition to changing, you'll also gain and lose followers. It's a really good idea to check in on your insights every few months and use that information to readjust the times you post.

## CONSCIOUS COLLABORATIONS

While being known for my cautious approach, I also know when to be a risk taker—which is crucial in today's ever-changing business world. On social media especially, you have to jump on ideas and investments quickly. Trends don't stick around that long and neither do viral videos.

There's no point in shooting and releasing a video after a trend has died down. So, in learning that I have to sometimes make quick decisions, I'm always willing to invest in an idea or a growth opportunity (unless it immediately looks like a failure). However, first I'll run a risk analysis against my brand, which identifies any potential issues that could negatively impact my business.

Every decision is an investment of your time and money. Make sure it's working for you by establishing a metric you can use as a reference when you have to make a quick decision on an investment. Mine is simple; I ask myself three key questions:

1. Does this trend or investment align with my brand mission?
2. What is the potential benefit to my brand from investing in this opportunity?
3. Is this the best way for my brand to invest in this opportunity?

When the #InMyFeelingsChallenge started, I could have easily done it. But doing what others are doing isn't part of my brand. Instead, we got Shiggy to be one of the first guests on Judy Springer. I was able to leverage the trend by doing something that was in line with the Jesseca Dupart brand and which became pretty popular on its own.

Beyond collaborations, I'm always very selective about who I seek advice from regarding my business and my investments. If I'm creating a new product, the last thing I want is that product's details to get out. In cases like that, I may not talk to others at all. If I'm looking at an opportunity in an area I don't know much about, such my property investments and taxes, I'll talk to someone I trust. I ask people for second opinions only if they have more knowledge or experience than me in an area. However, when it comes to KHP, I know my vision and I don't seek a lot of feedback. Other people have a way of messing with your vision, even when they're trying to help. For questions about my business, I seek help from prayer.

## INFLUENTIAL INSIGHTS

Connecting with an influencer to increase your brand profile is a good idea, and it was one of the first things I did when launching KHP. To start, you can trade services. For example, I did people's hair for them to tag my profile or as payment for someone to shoot an ad.

Influencers' prices can range from $50 to more than $1 million, so if I'm going to invest in someone to promote my brand, I need to make certain that I'm getting a return on that investment. I look at the influencer's activity, engagement levels and even comments on their posts to see if he or she is someone I want to do business with. When you collaborate, that influencer will be connected to your brand, so be strategic when making a selection. Because you want to see if the person aligns with what you're trying to do, consider questions such as:

- Is he or she connecting with my target audience?
  1. For example, there are a lot of influencers but not all of their followers are potential KHP customers. There's no point advertising to people who aren't interested your product. Luckily for us, Miracle Drops has a broad audience so we aren't really limited in terms of who we can advertise to.

- Are the influencer's engagements high?
  2. Don't be fooled by follower numbers. If somebody has two million followers but only averages 20,000 likes, it's a sign that people aren't checking their posts.

- Are the influencer's comments aligned with my brand statement?
  3. There have been celebrities and influencers I've been interested in working with but have changed my mind when I saw their comments, how they post about products or their replies to comments. I'm not going to deal with you if you're swearing or using foul language that's disrespectful to someone. Now, this is just a personal preference. I know other brands are okay with shock advertising and the tough image is part of their brand. You'll have to draw your own boundaries around what is acceptable for you as a brand.

- Does the influencer engage with his or her posts?
  4. I try to respond to as many people as possible, especially those who direct message me. I also have some followers who always support me and leave comments, so I always try to respond to them. If I can do this much, I want the influencer I'm paying to do that as well.

On the other hand, when you're doing paid promotions, it's important to be available to answer any questions under that influencer's post. It's also a good idea to have your team readily available to answer questions. Start small with local influencers and use the barter system I mentioned. Don't go to larger influencers until you're able to handle the cost and demand that comes with it.

Open your eyes to influencers you may not have traditionally thought of. For example, if you're an urban brand, you don't have to stick to urban influencers. Also, if you're promoting hair, don't hire an Instagram model because she more than likely has more male followers. The influencer has to have real influence in your sector.

## BEING PRESENT: A NOTE ON MENTAL HEALTH

Putting yourself up on social media is a huge step. Some people eventually burn out and stop creating because they no longer enjoy it. Sometimes, influencers also feel like they are always online and have no more privacy. It's really easy to get caught up in the world of social media, and always needing to create something new and relevant. Social media followers can love you one day and hate you the next, or love you but still leave nasty comments that tear you down.

You have to decide as a person, not a brand, how much of you and your life you want to share. Your life includes your family, friends and the activities you love. It's important to draw the line between your personal and business profiles. Social media users always want to learn more about the people they follow, and it's easy to feel like you're obligated to tell them everything. It took me a while, but I've created my boundaries and I'm pretty good at keeping them. My personal relationships, for example, are private. These are parts of my life that are special and important to me and the people in it. So, I keep that away from social media as much as I can. No matter what though, I try to put out as many positive posts as I can, without being fake, because I know that's what my followers expect.

Some days you may even get people posting negative stuff about you on their page rather than yours. There will be people who will try to make you feel all sorts of ways, including bad about yourself. When that happens and it negatively impacts you, take a social media break and return only when you feel ready. You can also develop practices and techniques like I talked about in Chapter 6 to manage negative comments or people coming your way. Finding your personal way to deal may involve taking up a boxing class, meditating, or just screaming or crying it out. I pray for clarity when I see these hateful comments, asking God why the comment affected me and to grant me the strength to forgive and move on.

# Chapter 10

## DEAR FUTURE CEO

Throughout this book, I wanted to show you that launching your own business doesn't have to be scary. But more importantly, it isn't something you need permission to do. Trust your vision and the Lord to help you achieve your greatness. Listen, if I can do it then you can do it! There's nothing "extraordinary" about me. I was born into your average family, faced some challenges that made me stronger and ended up where I am because I believe in the Lord and His vision for me. When I was ready to receive His blessings, He piled them on me. In doing so, He gave me a purpose to share my knowledge and support others to rise up and claim their blessings.

If you take nothing else away from this book, I want you to remember that you are unique and special. The Lord is ready to provide whatever answer you're seeking. You just got to open yourself up, pray and seek His guidance.

**Some things you gotta remember:**

- You have to clear the way for your blessings: Some people aren't deserving of the blessings you're about to receive. The Lord will hold back those blessings until you remove those people from your life.

- You don't need permission: Your vision is your own and no one can tell you that it's gonna work or fail. Only you know that because only you see what the Lord has gifted you to see. Stop waiting for others to let you be amazing.

- Pray through the process: No matter where you are in life and what point you are at, the Lord is there with the answer. Trust Him to light your way when you are in darkness, and turn to Him in gratitude during the bright moments.

- Make your own destiny: This book and all the lessons in it are just tools to help you move forward. You gotta do the work yourself. Not everything that worked for me is gonna be right for you. Take the lessons, take the stuff that matters and create your business and your brand your way. You're the CEO, so lead the way to your vision.

- Don't make decisions grounded in fear: I have made decisions that I knew were wrong but was so scared that I went through with them anyway. Why am I telling you this? I want you to know that sometimes we make decisions that aren't right for us. You may know it as you're making the decision or it may take a couple of days for the fear to vanish and the impact of your decision to hit, but you'll know. A decision based in fear isn't one that's going to move you forward.

- Get your sh*t in place: I'm always shocked when people start a business without getting the basics in place. It would suck to invest a bunch of time developing a brand only to realize someone else has the Twitter name, Instagram handle or worse, the website address. Do you have all your business elements in line? Is your paperwork done and set up? Do you have all the legal paperwork? You company is only as resilient as its foundation, so make sure it's laid right!

- Research is queen: Nothing can sink a business faster than being unprepared. Do your research, create a viable product and understand your market. The more you know, the better you'll be positioned to take over the industry. I'm always watching, learning and understanding what my clients and followers are looking for now and how that changed from yesterday.

## GETTING DOWN TO BUSINESS

Get a pen and paper and write down answers to the questions below.

### Part A: Skills Measure

1. My friend(s) would say my best qualities are? (list at least three to five characteristics)
2. My friend(s) would say I'm good at? (list three to five skills)
3. I think I am really good at? (list three to five skills)

Write your skills and characteristics in a chart similar to this:

| What am I good at? | Where can I use it? | Can I make money from it? | Do I need any certifications / additional training/licensing to do it? | What is stopping me? | How can I address this barrier? |
|---|---|---|---|---|---|
| *E.g. Hair styling* | *Styling* | *Yes* | *Hair styling certification* | *Time and money* | *Scholarships/ part-time classes* |
| *E.g. Organization* | *Event planning/ marketing campaigns* | *Yes* | *Event management certification (not necessary)* | *No clients* | *Speak to the pastor at church and see if I can organize an event* |

### Part B: Goal Setting

When you've completed the chart in Part A, you'll notice you have a lot of skills you can monetize. Some are going to get you excited as you think about them. Focus on those. Take two or three of the skills you've identified and create a SMART-R goal for them.

Pick the skills that:
- get you excited to start;
- have barriers that you can easily address; and
- align with the future you have planned in your mind.

**Remember, SMART–R goals are:**

1. **Specific** - The goal is clearly defined.
2. **Measurable** - How will this goal help to measure the impact of your brand?
3. **Achievable** - What steps do you need to take to make this goal happen?
4. **Realistic** - Can you achieve your goal with the resources you have available?
5. **Time-based** - By when do you want to achieve the goal?
6. **Results** - What does achieving this goal mean for your brand?

**Part C: Hold Yourself Accountable**

What are you going to do to hold yourself accountable? Some ideas can include:

- create a system of rewards to keep yourself motivated; and
- find an accountability partner who will keep you motivated and accountable to your commitments.

## MY FINAL PIECE OF ADVICE

Starting something, anything, can be terrifying. Owning a business has so many ups and downs that you have to be prepared, daily, for the unexpected. When I wrote this book, I thought about showing y'all what a day in my life would be like but I knew that wasn't gonna work. My life doesn't follow a schedule and each day comes with a new crisis or challenge. Your new life will too. Embrace it as part of the journey.

I think everything happens for a reason and though not every experience is pleasant, they all set you on the path you need to be on. I don't regret anything because while some decisions may seem harsh and hard, as a CEO these are the types of decisions you have to make. Why keep people around who aren't willing to work with you or sacrifice but want to reap the benefits of your work? Be selective about who is moving forward with you. The people you take on the journey are the ones who are going to help shape and impact your vision and company. So, if they aren't fully on board then you're going to be focusing your energy on convincing them rather than working towards your future.

Everything the Most High has given me, from blessings to trials, has led me to the path I am on today. With each trial, He has built my emotional reserve and strength to help me level up and succeed. I know He isn't going to move me up a new level unless He has faith that I'm ready. Not only are the blessings bigger as you level up, so are the trials that will test your path and faith. If you're not moving forward, it may be because you're still clinging to relationships or a mindset that are holding you back. The Lord knew I was ready to receive more blessings because he saw my faith and commitment increase.

Deciding I wanted something better for myself came with those same doubts and fears you are facing. It's easy to look at every mistake or failure and think it's a sign you should quit. In reality, those are lessons to help you fly. Every step and misstep, every experience is equipping you to succeed and achieve your goals. The difference between a successful CEO and anyone else is that he or she kept going! The successful CEO listened, learned and changed things to create something amazing.

You have the tools and skills to build a life that's truly extraordinary and to bring to existence whatever dreams you have. Trust your personality, abilities and your knowledge. You are made up of a unique combination that no one else in this world possesses. Believe in all the beauty and gifts the Divine blessed you with, and you will succeed. I'm excited to know that one day you'll be here with me, changing the world.

As you grow and build your vision, I wish you luck and blessings.

*Love,*
**Jesseca**

# WHEN THE MIRACLE DROPS

# Jesseca Dupart
## - AUTHOR -

*Jesseca Dupart* is an American entrepreneur, CEO and activist for healthy hair care. She is most well known for her beauty empire, Kaleidoscope Hair Products. In 2013, Jesseca decided to advance her entrepreneurial career by running with her vision of launching a full hair care line into the digital stratosphere. Kaleidoscope Hair Products has attracted men and women of all ethnicities and hair textures with its top seller, Miracle Drops.

Jesseca is in a league of her own, utilizing one-of-a-kind branding strategies to market her products. These unique social media-driven campaigns have triggered exponential growth within her company. To date, she has attained her own fully stocked warehouse and surpassed more than 100,000 customers. Kaleidoscope has superseded $15 million in sales, and continues to grow by the day. In 2018, Jesseca expanded her portfolio by creating her realty company, Kaleidoscope Realty, and launching her first non-profit organization, Kaleidoscope Kares. That same year, Jesseca and a team of collaborators became the current Guinness World Record holders for the largest toy giveaway.

Jesseca's mission is to inspire others to exceed their own expectations. She lives and encourages others to live by the notion, "pray through the process".